Mending Broken Connections

10 Simple Strategies to Restore Communication in Relationships

DENISE HEALY, M.A.

Cedar Rose Publishing®

Healy, Denise

MENDING BROKEN CONNECTIONS: 10 Simple Strategies to Restore Communication in Relationships / Denise Healy. First Edition.

First Edition: February 2019

ISBN 978-1-7335620-0-3

Copyright © 2019
Cedar Rose Publishing®
www.DeniseHealy.com
www.Streets2Schools.com

Editor: Linda A. Schantz
Cover Design: Christy Collins

Printed in the United States of America
All rights reserved under International Copyright Law.

All rights reserved. No part of this book may be reproduced in any form or by any electronic or mechanical means, including information storage and retrieval systems, without permission in writing from the publisher, except by a reviewer who may quote brief passages in a review.

This book is dedicated to Lena and Ilana.

Two women beautiful inside and out.

Two women successful in their own right.

Two women I continue to serve.

I am blessed every day to be your mother.

I will love and cherish you always.

DISCLAIMER

The contents, such as text, graphics, images, and other material contained in the book, Mending Broken Connections ("Book") are made available by the author and publisher for educational purposes only as well as to give the reader a general understanding of the strategies and processes described. The Book is not intended to be a substitute for professional mental health advice, diagnosis, or treatment. By reading this book you understand that there is no practitioner-client relationship between you and the Book author or publisher.

The Book is not intended to be used as a substitute for competent mental health services from a licensed mental health professional. Always seek the advice of your mental health practitioner or other qualified health provider with any questions you may have regarding a mental health condition. Never disregard professional mental health advice or delay in seeking it because of something you have read in this Book. If you think you may have a mental health emergency, call your mental health practitioner or 911 immediately. Reliance on any information provided by the Book is solely at the reader's discretion and risk.

Every story in the book is a composite of several story examples. Each story is made up of disparate or separate people, places, situations, and/or elements. Names, characters, businesses, places, events, locales, and incidents described are either the products of the author's imagination or used in a fictitious manner to more fully illustrate the particular point discussed in the applicable chapter. Any resemblance to actual persons, living or dead, or actual events is purely coincidental.

Although the author and publisher have made every effort to ensure that the information in this Book was correct at press time, the author and publisher do not assume and hereby disclaim any liability to any party for any loss, damage, or disruption caused by errors or omissions, whether such errors or omissions result from negligence, accident, or any other cause.

ACKNOWLEDGMENTS

I would like to express my appreciation and gratitude
to several people, who, without their mentoring, counsel,
and editing skills, this book would have remained
an idea waiting to express itself.

Thank you to:

Steve Harrison, Martha Bullen, and the Quantum Leap Team;

> Responsible for coaching me through the publishing and publicity process.

John C. Maxwell and members of the JMT faculty and family;

> Responsible for training, coaching, and holding me accountable to my visionary dreams.

Christy Collins, Constellation Book Services;

> Responsible for the cover design.

Last, but certainly not least,

Linda Schantz, Editor;

> Who, from the beginning to the end of the book development process, walked with me, to complete this work. Linda artfully ensured the words on the page align with the communication intended.

CONTENTS

INTRODUCTION 3

Chapter 1:
ACTIVE LISTENING 5
It's All a Matter of Perspective

Chapter 2:
STATE THE NOT-SO OBVIOUS 19
From Thinking to Verbalizing

Chapter 3:
LET GO OF THE ROPE 33
Letting Go of Power and Control

Chapter 4:
THE "WHAT" QUESTION 45
Activate the Curious, Problem-Solving Center of the Brain

Chapter 5:
YOU ARE MORE IMPORTANT THAN THE PROBLEM 57
Define Your Relationship Intention and Priority

Chapter 6:
CLARIFY BOUNDARIES 71
Un-Muddle the Jumble

Chapter 7:
MOTIVATION 89
Find One Strong Reason to Act

Chapter 8:
CHOICES..105
Freedom in Options

Chapter 9:
HABITS 123
Break Old Ones; Create New Ones

Chapter 10:
FOCUS ON SMALL SUCCESSES 135
Take Care of Your Next Minute

CONCLUSION 153

References
About the Author
Notes

INTRODUCTION

What you hold in your hand is a candid and sincere guide to help you mend broken connections in your relationships.

When the connections in a relationship break, sparks have a tendency to fly. When a relational tug of war begins, you may find yourself on the opposite side of your loved one mentally, emotionally, physically, and spiritually. Instead of an agreement between you, now there is a lack of clarity. Where there was peace, tension moves in. Instead of standing together, you find yourself and your loved one facing off for a fight, each of you bracing for defense. The harmony of your relationship is thrown off by fiery thoughts, words, and actions. The way to repair the discord and damage from a heated exchange is not easy to see.

This book offers hope for you and your partner to regain the closeness you once felt. Its purpose is to give you tools to reduce the arguments that sometimes occur over even the smallest matters. The strategies contained in this text are offered to assist you and your partner in restoring your common values, beliefs, loving thoughts, and feelings.

I offer this book to you, drawing on my experience of close to four decades of teaching, mentoring, coaching, and counseling thousands of real people. Throughout my career, fieldwork with individuals from all walks of life has led me to these proven strategies that will mend broken connections in all types of relationships. Every day I am privileged to assist people who are seeking to better themselves by taking steps to make positive changes in their relationships as a result of the strategies offered here. I am committed to helping those who are seeking a way to reconnect with a loved one and arming them with the positive, social skills they need to bring harmony back into their lives.

I am most interested in your success. The purpose of this work is for you to learn how to yield positive outcomes and success in your relationships.

As you read through this book and start to gain insight as to why a particular strategy is essential, you'll notice that each chapter contains composites of real-life stories. These examples are shared to illustrate how simple it is to put the principle into practice. Many of the stories recount the exact moment when a person using the particular social skill described realizes their own success. It is vital to remember that small successes lead to a new measure of confidence. A step-by-step guide is offered on how to transition from understanding a strategy to taking specific action steps and turning that strategy into a positive habit in your life. Beyond the "why" each chapter ends with "how" to put the strategies into practice. As you practice a strategy again and again, it becomes a positive habit that leads to lasting change. You will learn how to actively listen, effectively perspective take, and verbalize what you are thinking.

This book is dedicated to helping you let go of the illusion of power and control over each other, activate your curiosity and problem-solving abilities, redefine your relationship priorities, and much more.

Approach the material and your growth with grace. Be gentle with yourself and your partner, as well as, your collective old patterns and habits. As each of you begins to change you will experience the quiet success that follows the effort to develop new healthy habits. Your relationship will shift. You and your partner will become more intimate. Your incremental successes will be influential in reinforcing your commitment to continue your work. Over time, your diligence to use the positive relational skills you have developed will lead to a measure of relationship restoration. You will look back with a pleasant surprise to find that old negative patterns and habits in the relationship are but a distant shadow of the past.

As you begin to apply these real-life-tested action steps to mend your broken connections, may your bonds be strengthened, and your partnership be restored.

—Denise Healy—
M.A. in Educational Leadership
M.A. in Psychology
M.A. in School Psychology

Co-Founder and Co-CEO of Streets2Schools, Inc., and author of **Christopher's Anger,** WPS Publishing, and a contributing author to the book, **Success Formula,** with Jack Canfield.

Chapter 1
ACTIVE LISTENING

It's All A Matter of Perspective

SAM'S STORY

"I don't always listen to my wife," Sam said to me in one of our recent sessions. "But it really is her fault that there's always such a mess around the house!"

In the time that I had worked with Sam, we'd both come to realize that he had a tendency to get overly stressed about what he considered "a constant mess" in his home. The problem started early in their marriage and had grown to epic proportions over time. Sam's wife, Susan, was at her wit's end. She didn't know how to handle Sam's overreactions to what seemed to be trivial to her, and the couple was at odds in their relationship because of it.

Sam's assessment that day during our session was correct. He didn't always listen to his wife. When he was stressed about the mess in their home, he went on an all-out campaign to "clean the place up." He put in a tremendous amount of effort to put things in order, but he never considered his wife's perspective. Poor Susan would come home exhausted from a long day at work to find that none of her personal items were where she had left them.

In Sam's haste to put things away, he would just stuff things into the nearest hideaway thinking he was doing Susan a favor. Days, or sometimes weeks later, Susan would find a treasured item tucked away in some random place. Susan would often find things like a hairbrush in a kitchen drawer, the children's clothing in the hall closet rather than in their bedroom dressers, or canned foods in the cupboard where they kept pots and pans instead of in the pantry.

While Sam went around muttering about how he really shouldn't have to do all the cleaning in the house, Susan just got more frustrated. She had tried to talk to Sam on many occasions, asking him nicely to put things away in certain places, but in Sam's haste to tidy up, he just wanted to get things out of sight. He didn't see the problem with just stashing Susan's things wherever it was most convenient at the time. *If she didn't like it, why couldn't she just put her own stuff away?*

The underlying tension this was causing in the marriage was building to open anger. Sam knew he needed to work on his broken connection with Susan, but he needed help.

JAKE'S MOVE BACK HOME

"My mom is always so tense around me," Jake explained. "I know she has some problem with what I've done, but I don't know what it is. All I get from her is the silent treatment."

Jake was in a bind because, at age twenty-five, he had lost his job and had to move back home. "It's gotten so bad, I don't even want to be in the same room with her anymore."

Jake and his mother ate breakfast and dinner together almost every day. They would prepare their meals together, and often his mother would ask Jake to do things to help. Sometimes she would ask him to bring her food from the refrigerator, to help cook ingredients, or to set the table. Jake was happy to follow through with his mother's requests silently. He would nod or say "Okay" and then do what she asked. He was careful to make sure he was helpful around the house and pulling his weight.

But then something would usually go wrong. For no apparent reason, Jake's mother would seem to get mad at him. He couldn't understand why this kept happening. He made sure he had done what she asked. But about halfway through preparing every meal, his mother would tense up and stop talking to him. The two usually ended up eating at the same table in complete silence. *What was her problem?*

Until Jake could find another job and get back on his feet, he knew he had to make this awkward relationship with his mother work. He just didn't know how to do it.

ACTIVE LISTENING

Neither Sam or Jake in the two previous stories understood the basics of active listening in their relationships. American psychologist Carl Rogers, Ph.D., a founding theorist of humanistic psychology, originated the term "active listening." Rogers's work was based on the writings of Abraham Maslow and his theory of human motivation that first appeared in a 1943 article published by the ***Psychological Review*** and further developed in his book, ***Motivation and Personality***. Maslow's "Hierarchy of Needs" model theorized that an individual's basic physiological, safety, love/belonging, and esteem needs must be met prior to that person being able to reach the highest level of needs, namely, self-actualization.[1,5,6]

Rogers expanded on Maslow's theories, and a new perspective on human nature was formulated. Rogers's client-centered therapeutic approach surmised that for people to "grow" and reach self-actualization, they need an environment that provides them with the core conditions of empathy, congruence, and unconditional positive regard.[3]

The "active listening" technique sets the stage for relational growth because it requires a collaborative effort in communication where the listener becomes as active as the speaker.

To provide an environment which meets the core conditions of empathy, congruence, and unconditional positive regard for the speaker, the listener must remain actively present.[7] The "active listening" strategy includes the listener acknowledging what he or she has heard by rephrasing and checking for full understanding of what is being communicated.[2,4]

To break the technique of active listening down into layman's terms, one needs only to examine the definitions of the two words.

» To be *active* is *to take action or become effective.* In a relationship, it means to be energetic or protective; to take an interest in someone or something other than one's self.

» *Listening* is not just hearing. Real listening is *the ability to receive and interpret messages that have been communicated accurately.*

As participants learn to put the two ideas together, a good working definition of active listening means *someone is effectively showing interest by conscientiously paying attention to the speaker, thereby accurately receiving and interpreting a thought or idea from someone other than themselves.*

PUTTING ACTIVE LISTENING TO WORK FOR YOU

Knowing about and understanding how active listening strategies work is far different than applying and using them consistently in real-life situations.

To accomplish active listening in the communication process, it is essential to consider and practice the following four principles:

1. Refrain from judgment, criticism, or blame.
2. Acknowledge the other person is valuable and worthwhile.
3. Stop, think, and rephrase a presented idea before moving on to another idea.

4. Communicate when you are able to be an active listener and when you're not.

REFRAIN FROM JUDGMENT, CRITICISM, AND BLAME

Thoughts travel quickly through our heads during a conversation. There are many times when someone else is talking, and before they finish communicating a complete thought, we make a judgment or form an opinion about what they are saying. We often draw conclusions before we fully understand, but at this stage of communication making a judgment is premature. Active listening requires us to remain focused on an entire thought or idea that is being conveyed.

Premature judgments can cause us to give unwarranted criticism. When we criticize, we assess the merits of what is being said with unfavorable thoughts and comments. Such criticism leads us to find fault with another person's reasoning and shuts down all communication. Active listening keeps us engaged as our partner shares their entire thought process—that is until we really see their point of view. This prevents us from making snap judgments, faultfinding, and blaming them for what went wrong before we see the whole picture.

There will always be disagreements between any two people regarding their thoughts and ideas, but arguments and conflicts do not diminish either person's point of view. Our differences are what make us unique individuals.

Our relationship connections are broken, however, when we switch from disagreeing to blaming someone else. If we do so, we are no longer communicating. We're merely looking for a way to hold the other person responsible for our difficulties. Placing blame causes us to inappropriately express our disapproval and look for something wrong or unsatisfactory with another person or their reasoning. In times of conflict, the best way to resist engaging in blame is to hold yourself responsible, truly listen to the other person, and refrain from looking for something wrong with what your partner is saying.

ACKNOWLEDGE THAT THE OTHER PERSON IS VALUABLE AND WORTHWHILE

It is vital for you to share your individual point of view; however, it is more important to acknowledge that the person you are speaking to is valuable and worthwhile.

Active listening requires you to put your partner and the conversation between you above all else. To acknowledge them means you are willing to recognize as fact or to admit the truth of something they might be saying. In the context of communication, your acknowledgment must be about the other person's value and worthiness to be heard. Again, you will not always agree, but it is important to accept each other's right to be heard.

When actively listening to someone else, whether they are a random acquaintance or a significant partner, how intently you each strive to acknowledge the other person's value will set the tone for your entire conversation.

STOP, THINK, AND REPHRASE A PRESENTED IDEA BEFORE MOVING ON TO ANOTHER IDEA

The three steps of "stop, think, and rephrase" are harder to accomplish than one might think. In the case of active listening, it is essential to stop all thoughts and discontinue any distracting behaviors of our own to be fully present for the speaker.

Once your partner finishes their thought, it is important to begin putting what they said into context. Thinking is merely the arranging of ideas in a pattern of relationship. For most of us, this arranging process happens quite quickly. Our thoughts create connections and jump rapidly from one idea to another. If our thinking process gets overloaded, reactive behaviors occur and short-circuit our communication. When we stop our own thoughts from flooding in while another is speaking and really think about what they are expressing, we are on our way to successful communication.

The next step of active listening—rephrasing—means to express the idea you just heard again, but perhaps in a different way. Rephrasing is key in accomplishing a few things:

› The person communicating an idea perceives an open and willing listener.

› It helps the listener to clarify the accuracy of what was heard, and

› When this type of healthy conversation is engaged in, both parties feel listened to, and negative reactive behaviors are reduced.

COMMUNICATE WHEN YOU ARE ABLE TO BE AN ACTIVE LISTENER AND WHEN YOU ARE NOT

There are times when it is not appropriate to talk, and certain times are better than others for active listening. Establishing a quiet time and place for quality active listening is best.

If, in the process of communicating, it is clear that one or both of you are unable to be a quality active listener, stop the process respectfully.

When someone is stressed, fatigued, or excited they are not able to listen as actively as they might desire. In situations like these, it is completely reasonable to ask your partner to give your communication a rest for a while. If this happens, both partners must be intentional about setting another time and place when you can both agree to resume a quality interaction.

SAM'S RESULTS

Sam knew he was causing undue tension in his marriage because of his lack of listening skills. He wanted to feel that he and his wife were a team, rather than opponents.

As Sam began to practice the skill of active listening, he began to see success. He shared what he had learned about the process with Susan. Sam was working on developing this new habit, but Susan's help was needed. He asked Susan if they could organize things around the house together when they were both free. Susan agreed. Not only did they begin to work together, the house got cleaned in half the time. They actually had fun taking care of things. Sam took the time to stop and listen to Susan when he didn't know where something belonged. As Susan directed him, Sam would rephrase what she said and then take action to put the item in its place. He embraced their real communication and made a positive experience out of cleaning time. At the end of each clean-up session, Sam and Susan marveled at how they hadn't argued or complained about each other.

Sam realized that his success was in being able to rephrase what Susan said. He also admitted that he picked up things and put them in random places because he really didn't know where they went. By actively listening to Susan, he learned where the items went, and she discovered she could help him without being frustrated or stressed. As he took time to stop, think, and rephrase what Susan said, it never even crossed his mind to blame her for the mess.

Sam described their new way of doing things, "We rallied, worked together, and got the job done. How sweet is that?!"

HARMONY IN THE KITCHEN

Jake's new-found communication skills also gave him immediate success.

As Jake committed to practicing active listening with his mother, the day started like any other day. The two of them were in the kitchen when Jake's mother asked if Jake could get the bacon out of the refrigerator and start cooking it.

Jake stopped, looked at her, and rephrased what she said, "You want me to get the bacon and cook it up? Okay." Then he went to the refrigerator, got the bacon, and started to fry it.

Just then the toaster popped. Jake's mother asked him to butter the toast.

Again, Jake rephrased, "You want me to butter the toast? Okay." And the toast was buttered.

Their conversation continued:

"Can you set the table?"

"You want me to set the table? Okay."

"Can you pour the orange juice?"

"You want me to pour the orange juice? Okay."

Once breakfast was prepared with both of them sitting at the table, Jake's mother began to cry.

Jake couldn't believe her reaction. "Mom, what's wrong?" he asked.

She looked up at him and said, "Son, this is the first time we've spoken in forever. It's the best conversation we've had since you moved back into the house. I don't know what's changed, but thank you."

Jake was taken aback. He had no idea his silence and one-word responses in the past had been interpreted as though he didn't value his mother and never listened to her. Jake went on to share with his mother how he was practicing active listening.

Weeks later, things were different. Jake really enjoyed helping his mother with meals. The tension between them was gone, and their relationship had been restored.

MAKE IT A HABIT
ACTIVELY LISTEN
STEPS FOR SUCCESS

After you have set your intention to actively listen, clearly define when and where you will practice. You may first want to employ this strategy without informing your partner. This will allow you to notice the difference in their reactions to your new behavior in a real-life situation.

In each interaction, focus on your successful use of the active listening principles and on the response of the other person.

You may prefer, however, to be more direct. If that is the case, ask your partner for permission to practice the different strategies to find out which one works best for both of you. Then you can establish agreements around the practice.

Set a beginning and an end time for the following exercises, and focus on the four points of active listening.

EXERCISE 1:
REFRAIN FROM JUDGMENT, CRITICISM, AND BLAME

Let your partner know you are focusing on refraining from judgment, criticism, and blame.

» Set a time frame of no more than fifteen minutes for this exercise.

- On a sheet of paper draw four columns.
- Head each column in the following way:
  - Judgment
  - Criticism
  - Blame
  - Overriding idea
- Have your partner begin sharing an idea or issue.
- Focus on exactly what your partner is saying.
- Monitor your thoughts closely.
- Each time your mind wanders during the discussion, note if the notion that entered your mind is a judgment, criticism, blame, or an overriding idea. Indicate what the thought was with a tick mark in the appropriate column.
- Now change roles with your partner.
- While you share an idea or issue, have your partner actively listen.
- Have your partner record when their mind wanders and in which direction.
- When the set time is concluded, stop and compare notes.

EXERCISE 2:
ACKNOWLEDGE THAT THE OTHER PERSON IS VALUABLE AND WORTHWHILE

You may do this exercise without alerting your partner, or you may choose to let your partner know you will be focusing on acknowledging them as valuable and worthwhile for a week.

- Set your intentions on how many times a day for the next seven days you will reinforce your partner's value and worthiness.
    - Two times a day
    - Three times a day
    - Four or more times a day
- Determine what you are going to say to reinforce your intention. Some examples include:
    - *You mean the world to me.*
    - *I appreciate you.*
    - *I love you very much.*
    - *You add value to my life.*
    - *I appreciate your quality of character.*
    - *Thank you for loving me.*
- Determine if you will do something physically while you verbally reinforce your intention, such as:
    - Hold hands with your partner.
    - Give them a hug.
    - Stroke their arm, cheek, or hair.
    - Whisper in their ear.
    - Gaze directly into their eyes.
- At the end of the week, check in with your partner to review their response to your efforts.

EXERCISE 3:
STOP, THINK, AND REPHRASE A PRESENTED IDEA BEFORE MOVING ON TO ANOTHER IDEA

Let your partner know you are focusing on stopping, thinking, and rephrasing their presented idea before moving on to another idea.

- » Set your intentions on how many times a day for the next seven days you will stop, think, and rephrase a presenting idea before moving the conversation forward.
    - › Once a day
    - › Twice a day
    - › Every time you have a conversation

At the end of the week, check in with your partner to review their response to your efforts.

EXERCISE 4:
COMMUNICATE WHEN YOU ARE ABLE TO BE AN ACTIVE LISTENER AND WHEN YOU ARE NOT

Let your partner know that for the next seven days you will be focusing on communicating when you are able to be an active listener and when you are not.

- » Establish a quiet time and place for quality active listening each day.
- » Have an exit strategy that you both can agree upon.
- » If it is clear that one or both of you are unable to be a quality active listener, stop the process respectfully.
- » During each discussion, make sure to honor the designated stop time.
- » If you are both ready to communicate, but the practice becomes frustrating, acknowledge what you are feeling, and

communicate that you are unable to be an active listener in the moment.

» Then, set a time with your partner to practice again.

Chapter 2
STATE THE NOT-SO OBVIOUS

From Thinking to Verbalizing

DAVIE'S MUDDY, FILTHY, DIRTY HANDS, FACE, SHOES, AND SHIRT

"Get those shoes off!" Brian barked from the couch as Davie dropped to the floor to watch television. "If I've told you once, I've told you a thousand times. Take your muddy shoes off before you come in the house!"—Then, Brian added, just for good measure, "And your room is a filthy mess!"

Davie sank into himself as he unlaced his shoes, pulled them off, and walked over to drop them in the shoe bin by the door. As he started to step back into the living room to watch the rest of his television show, his eyes caught Brian's for a split-second, and that stopped him dead in his tracks.

Brian seized upon the opportunity and pounced. "The next time you come to the table, young man, I expect you to come with clean hands and a clean face. And make sure you don't spill anything else on that dirty, old shirt of yours."

With that, Davie turned on his heels to slink silently away to his room with his head hung in despair. The door closed behind him, and Brian was left standing all alone.

As Brian and I were talking, he shared this story with a measure of sadness. He knew he was overly harsh with Davie. He had the sense that he could do better to help his son develop healthy habits of self-care. Brian couldn't understand why he always reacted harshly when he saw Davie. It seemed as if Davie's mere presence pushed all the wrong emotional buttons and made Brian fly into a tirade of threats and putdowns toward his son.

Brian wanted his son to develop better habits of hygiene. He wanted Davie to take responsibility for himself. He couldn't understand why Davie didn't seem to understand what he wanted him to do. It was like there was some missing connection in Davie's mind that kept him from getting it. At first, Brian tried to ignore the messiness. He thought Davie would snap out of it in time, but Davie's behavior had only gotten worse. Brian didn't know how to get through to Davie, so he would yell and string a long list of violations at his son. When Davie deflated and folded in on himself, Brian just increased the volume to try to get the message through loud and clear.

What was it going to take?

BETH AND THE BOSSY NEIGHBOR

Beth didn't know Sara that well, but she always seemed friendly when they happened to see each other as they were coming and going from the apartment building where they both lived. One night after work, Sara invited Beth to join her at a local book club she frequented. Beth was the quiet type, and she had a hard time expressing herself, but she loved to read. Beth thought joining a book club might be the perfect way for her to find new and interesting friends. Maybe the club might help her to open up to people by talking with them about their shared love of books. Beth agreed to meet Sara outside the next evening so that they could ride together to the club's meeting place.

The next night, Beth met Sara outside their apartment building right on time. Sara volunteered to drive to the community center for the meeting, and the two young women walked to Sara's car in the parking lot.

"Put your seatbelt on," Sara barked before Beth even sat down. Beth quickly complied with Sara's request.

"You didn't eat anything before we left, did you?" Sara asked Beth impatiently.

"No, you said there was food at the club, so I didn't think I should eat anything," Beth replied.

Sara frowned a bit as she started the car. "Could you move your arm off the center console?" she asked. "I need space to drive."

Beth mumbled an apology and moved her arm right away.

About a mile down the road, Beth took out her compact mirror and lipstick. But before she could even open her lipstick, Sara barked at her again. "Don't do that. I don't want you to get makeup all over my car."

Sara spoke as though Beth were an unruly child. The farther they traveled, the louder and more demeaning Sara's comments became.

Beth's frustration grew with every mile, yet she struggled with her ability to communicate her feelings. In the past, whenever Beth's frustration level was running high, she found she wasn't good at expressing her feelings. She always got flustered and tended to bounce back and forth from one topic to another trying to communicate why she was upset. There were many times when she couldn't even finish a sentence before her mind made another jump. Most of the time in a heated discussion, Beth ended up not making any sense all—not even to herself. The car ride with Sara reminded Beth of how stupid and humiliated she felt every time she had to handle a conflict.

The next night, in our group session together, Beth shared that she had always preferred to "stuff" her feelings rather than embarrass herself in that way. Beth explained that she knew she was stuck for the evening. As Sara and Beth finally arrived at the book club that night, Beth's anxiety climbed. Beth did meet a couple of nice older women, and she enjoyed the club discussions about the book, but in the back of her mind, all Beth could focus on was how she was going to survive the long car ride home.

MOVING FROM THINKING TO VERBALIZATION

It is one thing to think something and quite another to speak your thoughts about a matter in a way that clearly communicates what you're thinking to those around you. Brian struggled to communicate clearly and parent his son Davie. Beth was unable to speak and stuffed her feelings and reactions to Sara's controlling behavior. The skill of moving from thinking to effective verbalization requires development.

The noted Swiss psychologist Jean Piaget surmised that adults are conditioned from childhood to think socially.[1] Mental images in the form of pictures, thoughts, and ideas run continuously through the mind in the attempt to communicate verbally. The inner speech of a man—what he says to himself—tends to run through hypotheses and forms possible conclusions before actual verbalization. This internal process takes place in preparation for the actual communication with others so that, when a thought is verbalized, the listener can understand what is being said. Piaget believed that the more developed a person's line of thought, the better able he or she would be to make him or herself understood. This internal thought process prior to verbalization also assists a person in the understanding of an alternative point of view.

Early studies of the connection between thought and language surfaced in 1962 by psychologist Lev Vygotsky. In his work, **Mind in Society,** Vygotsky argued that the mind could not be understood in isolation from its surrounding society or language.[2] In a modern take on the subject, psychologist Gary Lupyan discussed the point of view that normal human cognition is language-augmented cognition. He focused on the use of words as symbolic cues—and argued that language acts as a high-level control system which sculpts the human mind.[3]

QUALITY EXPRESSION

As internal dialogue and actual verbalized language shape our thoughts, we must be conscious of the concept that what we may be thinking is not what our partner may have in mind. We must learn to communicate the "not-so obvious" to others to help them understand our point of view, and we must listen without pre-suppositions of what we think they may think, feel, or believe. We need to get past the simple one-way expression of our thoughts and desires and move into *'quality expression,'* where both parties in the conversation understand what the other is saying.

The skill of quality expression is the ability to communicate your meaning and feelings in words with clarity and excellence. To achieve quality expression when communicating it's important to remember the following four keys:

1. Stay on one topic at a time.
2. Your personal beliefs drive your thoughts and ideas.
3. Be aware of personal expression through the senses, and
4. Say what you mean, and mean what you say.

STAY ON ONE TOPIC AT A TIME

Have you ever started a conversation with one idea or train of thought, and, by the time you finished, four other subjects or ideas had come up? The conversation began with a simple comment made about something that happened. Then, before you realized it, other observations, feelings, and random thoughts started pouring into the conversation pipeline backing up the flow of communication.

Last week when we were at the mall... And at your mother's house... When the kids were home... Remember yesterday?

Not only do we confuse our friends and loved ones, but also we create chaos in our own minds when we are unable to stay on one topic at a time. At the speed of thought, we can find ourselves in an entirely different place than where we were when we first started in any conversation. We can all think of a time when we had so much on our minds that it was difficult to prioritize our thoughts or even to sleep. The list of unfinished tasks at work, the needs of others in the house, and the outstanding inside and outside chores that require completion can cause us all to lose focus from time to time.

Staying on the topic takes effort, but once this skill is practiced, communication begins to flow effectively, and a whole lot of things begin to get done!

The easiest way to develop the skill of staying on topic is to practice three steps:

1. State the topic, subject, or idea, then take a deep breath.
2. While breathing in, restate the topic, subject, or idea in your head.
3. While you are exhaling, become aware of your listener and check to make sure they are actively listening to you.

This three-step process can seem awkward at first; however, once practiced, the process allows for the clear, quality expression of one subject at a time and keeps the conversation on track.

YOUR PERSONAL BELIEFS DRIVE YOUR THOUGHTS AND IDEAS

No matter who you are or what your background is, your personal beliefs drive your thoughts and ideas. A belief is a conviction that something is true. For example, a daughter may hold the belief that her mother will always care for her, or a son may believe his father will teach him about self-care. Whether they are factual or not, your internal beliefs shape your thoughts and direct the pattern of ideas that run through your mind. Your own beliefs and thought patterns naturally shape your ideas or mental images and concepts.

A father may think that all parents are loving, patient, and kind based upon his experiences observing five other families with children over a long period of time; however, his wife may have a completely different pattern of ideas than he does. Her concept of parenting may be in complete opposition to her husband's. If she grew up in a highly authoritarian family, she may not be able to see eye to eye with her husband on when or how their children should be disciplined. Their different beliefs will strongly impact their mental images and thought patterns and may result in significant conflicts between them.

As one might imagine, the concept of each person's beliefs driving their patterns of ideas strongly influences quality expression when two people are trying to communicate. Often communication is hindered because one person is trying to express what he or she believes to be absolute truth, but, from the listener's vantage point, the thought being communicated isn't truth at all.

The key to remember here is that your beliefs are shaping your thoughts, but your beliefs are just that—***your*** beliefs. If your partner does not share your beliefs, and you don't feel as if you are getting through, the best thing to do is to step back and reevaluate your personal convictions. As you take time to reevaluate why you believe what you believe and how those beliefs are shaping your mental images of the truth, the opportunity for a change in thought patterns will avail itself.

BE AWARE OF PERSONAL EXPRESSION THROUGH THE SENSES

We are sensory beings who receive information through all of our senses, and, as such, we express information from our senses continuously.

As you try to capture the quality expression you seek with another person, it is essential to be aware of your facial expressions and body posturing. This is very important because the person you want to communicate with may have a reaction to a particular look on your face or a stance you may take and not be available to you as an active listener. Rejection will occur before any idea has been shared.

As you begin to communicate, also take note of your voice tone, volume, and language. Communication gets lost when voice tone is harsh, words are screamed, or profanity is used. When these behaviors are present, a listener will become reactive to the way in which the idea is being shared. Even though your partner may have no issues with the idea itself, if you've presented it in a way that seems threatening with your body language or voice tone, your communication will be hindered. A calm presentation of your thoughts or ideas allows for effective personal expression.

SAY WHAT YOU MEAN AND MEAN WHAT YOU SAY

Wanting others to listen and actually *having* them listen are two different things. People listen to others who demonstrate that they have these three essential qualities:

1. Integrity—wholeness, completeness, and/or moral soundness

   An example of this might be when a mother teaches her children to tell the truth in every situation, regardless of the consequences.

2. Dependability—reliability and trustworthyness

   When the nieces and nephews go to Uncle Wally for advice, they can always trust that he will listen to them.

3. A measure of Accountability and Follow Through—the quality of being bound to give an explanation for actions and doing what you said you would do

Anne holds herself to a higher level of accountability now that she has a child.

A person who attempts quality expression in communication can be relied upon. He or she becomes the go-to person for information and counsel. Trust between two people is developed when each party takes the time to explain what they mean fully and follows through with their promises.

BRIAN'S RESOLVE

Through our discussions in my office, Brian came to realize that he had never actually verbalized to Davie his expectations concerning Davie's daily self-care and hygiene habits. He was clear in his head about what he expected. It seemed evident to Brian what his son should do, but it wasn't obvious to Davie. Brian assumed Davie knew what he wanted, but Brian had never shared these expectations with Davie.

After he came to this realization, Brian committed to helping his son develop healthy habits. He took Davie aside and apologized for being so harsh. He explained that he wanted to teach Davie why it was important to place his muddy shoes in the bin at the front door when he came in each day. Brian focused on the topic about where Davie's shoes belonged until Davie was able to communicate back that he understood.

Then the two of them took the conversation a step further. Brian and Davie brainstormed about ways Davie could remember to take off his shoes at the front door each day. "We could put a big note on the door for me!" Davie suggested.

"Or how about getting a doormat with big footprints on it?" Brian countered. Brian sensed the fun and play in the exchange, and both father and son laughed.

At the end of the conversation, Brian shared that he would be monitoring his son's ability to meet his expectations. By the end of the week, Davie was fulfilling his father's expectations every time he came into the house.

After that small encounter, Brian began to gain his parental confidence in setting and teaching his son to meet his expectations. He was able to address each personal hygiene issue, one at a time, in the same manner as he had about the muddy shoes. Before long, Brian had no more harsh words for his son, and Davie no longer retreated into himself or felt as if he needed to slink into his room with his head down. Brian's expectations were clear, and Davie met them on a regular basis. He and his father were finally able to share the living room and watch Davie's favorite television program or a ball game together, laughing and enjoying each other's company.

And if Davie happens to forget what is expected of him, Brian knows that all he has to do is remind his son of their conversation on the matter, and Davie will respectfully respond.

BETH'S COURAGEOUS PLAN

Beth and I discussed her situation from the night of the book club meeting. Beth shared that she liked the women in the book club and sincerely wanted to keep attending the meetings. But she didn't want to ride with Sara anymore. Beth expressed to me that she was very anxious about having to tell Sara she wanted to drive to the meetings on her own. Beth didn't want to lie to her neighbor. She didn't know how to express the real reason for her wanting to drive in a separate car while remaining in the book club. She wasn't sure how she could stay in the group without feeling anxious about facing Sara each week.

As we dug deeper into Beth's fears, I explained a three-step strategy of how to stay focused on one topic during any verbal conflict. Beth immediately decided that she wanted to put the three steps into practice. That evening, she invited Sara to walk to the neighborhood bistro with her for a cup of coffee. Beth engaged in small talk with Sara for a few minutes until she could muster the courage to say what she wanted to say. Then at the coffee shop, Beth dove into her topic.

"Hey Sara, just so you know, I'll be taking my own car to the next book club meeting." Beth took a deep breath and, in her head, repeated the statement to herself. *I will be taking my own car to the next book club meeting.* Beth watched Sara and checked to see if she was actively listening.

"Okay," Sara replied. "Do you have time to take a walk before heading back to the apartment?"

Beth was caught off guard. She didn't know what to expect from Sara, but it certainly wasn't compliance or an invitation to continue the visit with a walk. There was no push back, no drama. Beth was a bit confused by Sara's response, but she was also very relieved. Beth was prepared for an ugly conversation, but that didn't happen. Beth was able to stay on the one topic, express herself with one sentence, and then move on.

Beth was also caught off guard by Sara's ease in accepting the fact that Beth wanted to drive alone to the next meeting. She had wrongly assumed Sara would push back and make a scene. When she didn't react the way Beth had expected, Beth had a moment to reevaluate her beliefs about Sara.

Beth had been ready to end their friendship before it had even begun. When there was no drama, Beth had to change her initial assessment of Sara's character.

"Sure. A walk sounds nice." Beth responded.

The two women picked up their coffee cups and headed to the nearby park to visit the rose garden. As they walked, Beth realized she had a new-found respect for Sara. Beth knew she wasn't going to change Sara's bossy behavior in the car, but Beth had hope that perhaps, as they got to know each other better, she might be able to address the topic without feeling anxious. *But for now,* she thought to herself, *a walk and the smell of roses would do.*

MAKE IT A HABIT
STATE THE NOT-SO OBVIOUS
STEPS FOR SUCCESS

After you have set your intention to express yourself and turn your thoughts into words, clearly define when and where you will practice. For this exercise, you may first want to employ this strategy without informing your partner or friend. As with the other strategies, this will allow you to notice the difference in their reactions to your new behavior in a real-life situation. In each interaction, focus on your successful use of the expression principles and on the response of your partner.

If you decide that the direct approach may be more advantageous, let your partner or friend know you are attempting to practice expressing yourself better through clear verbalization of your thoughts. Ask for their support as you practice. Set your intentions each time you practice the strategies for quality expression then focus on the four exercises in the process.

EXERCISE 1:
PICK AND STAY ON ONE TOPIC AT A TIME

» State the topic, subject, or idea.

» Take a deep breath.

» While breathing in, restate the topic, subject, or idea in your head.

» While you are exhaling, become aware of your listener, and check to see if they are actively listening.

» Practice this exercise for a week. Log your awareness and success.

EXERCISE 2:
EXAMINE YOUR BELIEFS THAT ARE DRIVING THE SINGULAR TOPIC, THOUGHT, OR IDEA BEFORE YOU BEGIN COMMUNICATING

- » What is the basis of your point of view?
- » Why is this topic, thought, or idea important to you?
- » Practice this exercise for a week. Log your awareness and insights.

EXERCISE 3:
BE AWARE OF PERSONAL EXPRESSION THROUGH THE SENSES

- » Note your facial expressions and body posturing.
- » Note your voice tone, volume, and language.
- » Practice this exercise for a week. Log your awareness and insights.

EXERCISE 4:
SAY WHAT YOU MEAN AND MEAN WHAT YOU SAY

- » Set your intention with integrity, dependability, and accountability.
- » You may even want to rehearse your thoughts to yourself or out loud.
- » Practice this exercise for a week. Log your successes.

Once you have practiced the exercises separately, try practicing them simultaneously, two at a time or all of them together. Evaluate your success. Did you find the process easy? Could you have moved on to sharing a second topic easily, or was it best to end after the first sharing?

Becoming proficient with this strategy varies for each person. Some people, such as Brian, can pick the strategy up and put it into practice very quickly. Others, such as Beth, need a little more time practicing putting their thoughts into words before they are comfortable in every situation.

Chapter 3

LET GO OF THE ROPE

Letting Go of Power and Control

JOE'S ROCKY MARRIAGE

I had been working with Joe for a few months. His marriage was on the rocks. During one of our counseling sessions, I asked him, "What do you love about your wife?"

Joe hesitated. Then he shared with a heavy heart, "I can't say. I don't think I even like Ellen anymore." Joe's sadness was palpable. He and his wife had been married for five years. According to Joe, the fighting started during their honeymoon and never stopped.

Joe knew he sometimes stirred up the negative energy in his marriage. He readily admitted to me that he was partly to blame for the arguments. He had a quick temper and a nasty mouth. When things got heated between the couple, Joe usually resorted to yelling at Ellen and calling her vile names.

But make no mistake; Ellen was not a doormat. She knew how to use every trick in the book to her advantage. If she wasn't happy with something, she let Joe know it by nagging and yelling at him. If things really got heated between the pair, sometimes Ellen would verbally assault Joe and throw in a string of profanities for good measure.

Ellen and Joe fought as if each of their lives depended upon winning. Their reactionary behavior toward each other kept them stuck in an unhappy relationship full of conflict. Neither of them wanted a separation, but they weren't sure they could stay together much longer.

TAMMY'S EX

Divorce was never in Tammy's life plan. Her first husband, the love of her life, had died in an accident. Tammy was devastated for herself and their daughter. A few years later, Tammy married for a second time. This relationship became unmanageable soon after the wedding day. A cycle of verbal abuse and physical violence became a part of the couples' daily lives. Over the next few years, and during make-up phases of the cycle of violence, Tammy had three more children. All the while the couple was in a perpetual war.

Finally, six years in, Tammy mustered the strength to end the marriage. Slowly she began to gain inner strength and heal. She learned healthy self-help and parenting skills from a local divorce-recovery support group. Tammy worked hard at applying what she had learned. She was determined to live a violence-free life with her children. Tammy and her children were thriving with the positive changes she had put into practice.

Yet, Tammy's ex-husband remained invested in perpetuating the violence. He went to court to gain joint custody of the children. At face value, the judge saw nothing wrong with the request. Joint custody was granted. The judge's one stipulation was that both parties would go to mediation to resolve contested issues around parenting.

At mediation Tammy and her ex were civil. It was only after they were out of earshot of the mediator that Tammy's ex-husband would pick up an imaginary rope and attempt to engage her in a tug of war. He often threatened her with violence, called her a bad mother, and said that someday he would be taking their children away from her for good.

One day Tammy was tested. It was her week to have the children, and she arrived to pick them up at her ex-husband's house only to find they were not there. Tammy panicked because she didn't know what to do. Her ex was not answering her calls. A day went by without any communication from him or her children. Days turned into weeks, and Tammy was frantic.

IT'S ALL PART OF THE GAME—OR IS IT?

Joe and Tammy were in a tug of war within their respective relationships. Tug of war is a well-known rope game. As with most rope games, tug of war is based on some common agreement about the rules. First, two teams are picked with an agreement to balance out the people on each team in terms of number, gender, strength, and size. Then a centerline is clearly marked on the ground. Next, the winning lines are designated ten or more feet on either side of the centerline. The rope is marked with a center streamer that hovers over the centerline at the start. Finally, a designated judge is selected to monitor the game. The judge holds the responsibility to enforce the agreed upon rules and to watch for rule breaches.

As the game begins, teams line up on either side of the centerline, space themselves apart evenly, and pick up the rope. The clock is set at fifteen minutes. As the starting whistle blows, each team pulls on the rope as hard as they can. The goal is to pull the center streamer over one of the winning lines on the ground, and a winner is declared.

Tug of war in a relationship is another thing altogether. It is not a game. In a relational tug of war, there are no agreements and no rules. There are no real or perceived centerlines or winning lines designated, marking clear boundaries. There isn't even a streamer in the middle to indicate who won at the end.

In a relationship tug of war, two people face off, positioning themselves on opposite sides of each other mentally, emotionally, and physically. Instead of agreement, there is a lack of clarity, and there is tension and bracing for defense. More often than not there is an imbalance in terms of gender, strength, and size. There is no designated judge to monitor exchanges and hold each party accountable to the rules of civility.

In a relationship tug of war both people are compelled to pick up their ends of an imaginary rope. One person will usually pick up their end first as they try to gain control over their partner. The first person may say or do something that triggers the other one to take the bait and engage. Both parties end up holding opposite ends of the proverbial rope, pulling against each other as hard they can. The goal becomes to win by any means possible. Tension builds, momentum spirals high, and the situation becomes detrimental to the relationship and to the individuals involved.

LET GO OF THE ROPE

Our brains are hardwired to regulate attention, emotion, and morality, and to problem solve through the anterior cingulate cortex (the "ACC"). This complex part of the human brain is vital to our autonomic functions such as breathing and heart rate. According to noted researcher James Michael Hyman, one function of the ACC is to create our mental expectations about future experiences.[1] Hyman postulates that when the real-life experience we were focused on actually happens, our brains quickly evaluate if our predicted expectations match the current real outcome. If there is a discrepancy between our expectations and reality, the ACC reacts with a greater electrical charge. Hyman describes this jolt to our brains as "feedback negativity."

Identifying this feedback negativity begs the question, "Do we have any control over this electrical charge and our ability to change how we regulate attention, emotion, morality, and problem-solving?" Research indicates that indeed we do. Qualities such as emotion regulation can be cultivated and can actually change the mind and brain.[2]

The concept behind the "Let Go of the Rope" strategy is to help individuals let go of power and control in an argument—to resist the negative jolt of feedback coursing through their brains. The idea is to loosen your grip and release your end of the imaginary rope. As you extricate yourself from the negative interaction of an emotionally charged situation, you are able to disengage from the tension of the moment and focus on the underlying issue of concern. When you release yourself—first within your mind, then through your actions in the moment—you will experience a sense of freedom and emancipation from the unhealthy and/or potentially violent exchange.

The idea is that if we plant seeds through the understanding and application of specific strategies like "Let Go of the Rope," we can strengthen the ACC, the key part of our brains, where social awareness emerges, moral reasoning and decision making takes place, and where compassion forms. As we practice releasing control in our relational conflicts, we can actually train our brains to begin to form new, more positive patterns of behavior. The more we employ these relational skills, the better we will become at performing this positive practice over time and creating a new and automatized habit.[3,4]

PUTTING THE CONCEPT TO WORK FOR YOU: SIX KEYS TO LETTING GO OF THE ROPE

To practice the strategy of letting go of the rope to try to mend a broken relationship, it's important to remember and practice the following six keys:

1. Set your intention.
2. Clearly define the issue.
3. Ask permission to discuss the issue.
4. Establish agreements.
5. Set an end time.
6. Close with compassion.

SET YOUR INTENTION

Letting go of an imaginary rope of conflict is based on setting and communicating your intention. One or both parties must intentionally decide to use the strategy when it becomes apparent a tug of war is about to ensue. Preferably a couple will practice the strategy together, though, one person can use the strategy while being a living example to their partner. In any case, all things must start by having a clear intention.

CLEARLY DEFINE THE ISSUE

Determine the purpose of the conversation and do not stray from it. One issue in Joe's case was the equitable distribution of chores around the house. In Tammy's case, the primary issue was peaceful co-parenting while being divorced. Be clear in your mind what it is that you want your partner to know and understand.

ASK PERMISSION TO DISCUSS THE ISSUE

There are better times than others to discuss important issues in a relationship. You may be ready to talk about a pressing topic, but your partner may busy, tired, or unavailable. Remain flexible and considerate of your partner's availability and timing. Determining, *If not now, when?* is important to ensure an eventual resolution to the matter.

ESTABLISH AGREEMENTS

Determine where you want to have the conversation. You might want to talk at the kitchen table, outside on the porch, or on the couch. Sitting on the bed facing each other might be preferable. Review and agree to the rules of the strategy before you begin the discussion. Agree to self-monitor and take responsibility to hold each other accountable for enforcing the agreed upon rules. Agree to be quiet when you notice your partner has breached a previously determined rule. Allow them the time and space to acknowledge and assume responsibility for the breach. If you violate any of the agreements, humble yourself, apologize, let go of the imaginary rope, and continue the discussion if your partner is willing and able to do so.

SET AN END TIME

In the beginning, when you and your partner are just learning and practicing the strategy, set the clock for no more than fifteen minutes. You both want to experience success with the strategy the first time trying it. Know going in that there may not be a resolve to the intended issue the first time you practice. That's okay. The goal is not to win. It is to imagine letting go of the imaginary rope and remain calm while listening and expressing yourself.

CLOSE WITH COMPASSION

When the timer buzzes after fifteen minutes, stop the interaction. Agree to end the communication amicably with kind words, hand holding, and/or a hug. After a healthy close to the discussion, get up and go in separate directions. It is a good idea for each of you to sit alone and reflect on your exchange. You may want to contemplate the event or write your thoughts down in a journal. Focus on your success with the strategy and on areas that may require improvement.

A WORD OF CAUTION

"Letting go of the rope" the first time in a heated conflict can be disorienting. It can cause you to lose your bearings and experience confusion. It may cause feelings of embarrassment or wounded pride. At first, it may even compel you to hold tighter to the imaginary rope. Experiencing the shift for the first time from a position of needing to gain power and control in an exchange at all costs to exercising the release of your power and control can cause surprise and shock to your thought processes and emotions.

JOE'S AND ELLEN'S SUCCESS

I shared the "Let Go of the Rope" strategy with Joe and asked if he would be willing to practice the technique with his wife. Joe was skeptical. He wasn't confident that he could pull off or even remember the strategy in the heat of one of their arguments, nor did he believe Ellen would respond favorably to his use of the strategy.

A few weeks later, Joe came to me and shared his success. He recounted his own shock and surprise, and the shock and surprise of his wife when he tried the strategy for the first time. Joe explained that he and Ellen had been in a heated argument. The emotional tug of war started over a few simple chores not being completed. Then Joe suddenly remembered what I had told him about letting go of the rope.

Joe was able to remain present and conjure up an image of himself holding on tightly to a rope. He visualized himself letting go and releasing the imaginary rope from his hands. Joe marveled at what came next. Instantly his hands dropped to his sides, and his body relaxed. He stared at his wife in silence as she continued the unhealthy verbal assault. He said nothing. None of the usual comebacks or profanities came to his mind. Joe's facial expression relaxed. He gave no indications of resistance or a struggle for power or control.

Joe shared that, in that moment, he felt oddly calm. In his mind he saw the dynamic of power and control between him and Ellen clearly for the first time. Joe was amazed at his ability to rein in his desire for power and control over the argument and his wife. For the first time, he was able to redirect his negative energies away from the person in front of him. He was successful at focusing and regulating his own reactions.

Ellen hesitated and froze in confusion. Joe was not pushing back, expressing his opinion, or reacting to her verbal assault. He was not yelling or calling her names. She pulled herself out of the conversation to mentally regroup and moved to another room in the house. No resolve to the underlying issue came that day; yet, both parties went their separate ways marveling at the calm moment in the eye of the storm.

Joe shared that, a few days later, he and Ellen were at it again. This time Joe was ready to build on his success and practice his new-found strategy. He was able to imagine the rope in his hands again. He was able to release the rope in his mind just as the exchange got heated. Joe was so amazed at the success of the strategy that he dropped and sat down on the couch. Ellen moved to stand over him trying to maintain the aggressive energy. Joe, once again, marveled at his own ability not to react. He showed no indication of resistance, power, or control.

"Joe, what are you doing?" Ellen asked.

"I'm releasing the rope!" He chuckled. "Look," he continued. "I'm interested in what you have to say. I just don't want to argue any more."

Ellen calmly sat on the couch beside Joe. For the first time in five years, they really talked. They listened to each other. They worked through the issue that concerned them both. Joe and his wife ended the conversation surprised at their ability to resolve something together.

Joe told me, "I felt a little confused about what to do next. At the end of it all, I took her hand and gave her an awkward hug. It was kind of like we were meeting for the first time all over again."

After Joe shared his success, I asked him the same question I had asked him three weeks before, "What do you love about your wife?"

Tenderly Joe responded, "I like how she comes up behind me and runs her hand down my back. I like how she whispers in my ear, 'Can we talk now?' I have always loved her smile and her hair."

I can say with a measure of confidence, Joe's success set in motion a new positive pattern of resolving issues in their relationship.

TAMMY'S VERDICT

After the police got involved, Tammy's ex-husband returned their three kids. He still taunted her and made threats whenever they had to interact. As she and I talked, Tammy realized there was no way for her to control her ex-husband's outbursts and dangerous behavior, and she also saw that she had to let go of her end of the rope to end the mental torment he was causing her.

Each time after that, Tammy was able to detach from her feelings of anxiety when she had to interact with her ex-husband. She imagined herself dropping her end of the rope on the ground and leaving it there. She became practiced at walking away from her ex without engaging in his vicious mind games.

Soon after that first major incident, Tammy gathered her wits and went to the court. She was able to get on the docket for a hearing. Tammy worked with her lawyer and the mediator to establish and defend her case. She would seek sole physical custody and allow only supervised visiting rights for her ex-husband.

This time at the hearing Tammy's ex-husband showed his true colors. First, he attempted to engage in a mental tug of war with Tammy, then with the mediator, then with the judge. None of them took the bait or were inclined to pick up the other end of his imaginary rope. During the entire trial, Tammy imagined the rope sitting coiled up at her ex-husband's feet. In her remarks to the court, she shared that all she felt was overwhelming sadness for this man she had once loved.

The ruling went in Tammy's favor. She was awarded sole custody of her children. She continued to imagine a coiled rope at her ex-husband's feet whenever he saw the children for visits. Through "letting go of the rope," Tammy has grown. An unexpected development has taken place in her heart, as well. Tammy has learned to replace her feelings of sadness with true compassion when her ex-husband is around.

MAKE IT A HABIT
LET GO OF THE ROPE
STEPS FOR SUCCESS

Set your intentions each time you practice the strategies for letting go of power and control. Then focus on the key points in the exercise.

EXERCISE 1:
PRACTICE LETTING GO OF THE ROPE

After you have set your intentions, clearly define the issue at hand. Ask permission to discuss the issue. Establish your agreements, and set an end time. Focus on the following.

- Imagine a thick rope coiled on the ground between you and your partner.
- Commit to not picking up your end of the rope.
- If your partner picks up their end of the rope from your point of view; thinking or speaking negatively, raising their voice, using verbal hostility, name-calling, profanity, or posturing:
  - Stop talking.
  - Relax your face.
  - Cast your gaze downward.
  - Wait for your partner to notice that you perceive them as picking up the rope.
  - Allow your partner time and space to acknowledge and assume responsibility for the breach.
  - Ask them to let go of the rope.
  - Allow your partner to take responsibility for humbling himself or herself, apologizing, and move on with the conversation.
  - If your partner is unable to assume responsibility, end the exchange amicably, and close with compassion.
  - Go your separate way.
- If you pick up one end of the imaginary rope; thinking or speaking negatively, raising your voice, using verbal hostility, name-calling, profanity, or posturing:

- Imagine yourself holding tight to your end of the rope.
- Imagine letting go of the rope.
- Allow yourself time and space to acknowledge and assume responsibility for the breach.
- Humble yourself, apologize, and move forward with the conversation.
- If you are unable to assume responsibility, agree to end the exchange amicably, and close with compassion.
- Go your separate way.

If you and your partner are able to reach the end of fifteen minutes successfully without struggling with power and control, celebrate! If you made small gains, celebrate! There will always be another issue to discuss. You are ready to close with compassion. Remember to leave your partner with kind words, hand holding, and/or a hug.

Chapter 4
THE "WHAT" QUESTION

Activate the Curious, Problem-Solving Center of the Brain

FRANK'S STRANGE NEW HABIT

"What?" Frank slapped his hand on his forehead a little too hard and squeezed his temples between his thumb and middle finger. *"What? What? What?"* he repeated as he pushed past his wife and went toward the bedroom.

Susie could hear Frank all the way from the kitchen. She had no idea why he kept asking *'what?'* and then mumbling something to himself.

In the bedroom, Frank changed out of his work clothes and showered. About twenty minutes later, all clean and ready, he came back into the kitchen. Still, he kept asking, *'what?'* Then, Frank shouted for the whole family to hear, "I can do this! I know I can do this!"

This odd behavior went on for about a week. Even though Susie was curious about Frank's strange new habit, she didn't dare ask him about it. She didn't want to jinx things. After Frank had made his proclamation to the world, *'I can do this! I know I can do this,'* Frank had started doing some random, but wonderfully playful and loving things. And Susie liked it.

One night he scooped Susie up in the middle of the kitchen, gave her a bear hug, spun her around, showered her with kisses, and complimented her on her cooking efforts. On another night, Frank turned off the TV right in the middle of the kids watching a show. Through the protests, he pulled out a board game and herded the kids around the coffee table to play. On another night he pulled Susie away from cooking dinner into their bedroom. He held her close and reminded her that she was the love of his life. He kissed her warmly then escorted her back to the kitchen to finish what she was doing.

Since Frank's strange behavior had first started, Susie had noticed there was less tension in the house. Frank didn't seem as disconnected or tired as he usually was. Evenings in the family's home were becoming less about TV and more about family time.

BRUCE'S TEMPTATIONS

Bruce first came to talk to me in mid-December. He shared that there were two men going around his neighborhood selling illegal fireworks. Bruce was tempted to buy some and throw a big New Year's celebration party in their backyard for his family. As the salesmen had pressured him to make a purchase, he thought to himself, *If I buy the big package deal, the boys could really end the year with a bang!* Bruce listened to the men describe the bottle rockets, brocades, cones, and confetti. Bruce imagined flashes of color in the sky ending with a barrage of exploding stars ejected from Roman candles set up all around the backyard. Not only would the boys be excited, the neighbors would also get a great show. Bruce was primed to buy an assortment of amazing fireworks for the low, low cost of only five hundred dollars.

Fortunately, though, Bruce's phone started ringing just before he agreed to the deal. It was Bruce's supervisor, and he quickly extricated himself from the hard sell because the call was urgent. As the two salesmen said they'd come back the next week to close the deal, Bruce realized he had literally been saved by the bell.

The next morning, Bruce made an appointment to see me because he knew he had to change his behavior. When we met, he shared with me how he struggled with his spontaneous impulses. He realized that acting on his temptations without first stopping to think about the repercussions was costing him a lot of money and time, and his relationships were suffering because of it. He described how, just the month before our conversation, there had been a puppy someone left in a box outside a store. Without even thinking, he scooped up the little fur-ball and took it home. He also told me that the week before that, his wife, Judy, had made an offhanded comment and said, "That shirt is cute," as they walked by a clothing shop in the mall. Bruce later circled back around and bought it to surprise her with the gift.

All of Bruce's actions were well intended, but they almost always had secondary consequences. The family already had two dogs and a cat when he picked up the last puppy, and, while the shirt was cute, and Judy really did appreciate the thought, the two-hundred-dollar purchase maxed out their only credit card. That money could have paid for two pairs of school shoes, one for their son Danny and the other for his brother, Tom. Bruce knew that Judy would come back to the mall on another day and return the shirt—and she would figure out a way to buy two pairs of shoes for the boys from a less expensive store.

Bruce's lack of self-control was causing a rift in his marriage. December wasn't a month to buy unnecessary things. Judy tightly budgeted the family's limited funds to pay for the mortgage, the car payment, the utilities, and food for the month. She had been scraping and saving a little money each month all year long so the boys would each get one nice gift they wanted for the holidays. Judy also made sure that there were a few small gifts for each child as well, all wrapped in holiday cheer. Bruce knew spending five hundred dollars on illegal fireworks for a big year-end bash was not in the family's budget.

His out-of-control spending wasn't the only reason Bruce's marriage was strained. His spontaneity at work was also draining the life out of his relationship with Judy. At work, Bruce interacted with people all day on his delivery truck route. The job required Bruce to drop his company's bottled soda products off at the back door of each convenience store on his route, get the delivery ticket signed, and then move on to his next stop. That's it. He was expected back in the yard between four and four-thirty each afternoon.

Judy expected Bruce to be home for dinner by five-thirty each night. Unfortunately, that wasn't usually what happened. Often, he would get requests from store owners to move product to their supply rooms or help stock their displays. When Bruce would spontaneously respond to these requests, the time would add up. He was adding one, sometimes two, hours to his schedule each day. Bruce's supervisors couldn't understand why Bruce was coming in from his routes at six or seven o'clock most evenings, but they didn't really care because Bruce got paid by the amount of product he delivered, not by the number of hours he worked. Meanwhile, Judy was at the house reheating the family meal almost every night. By the time Bruce made it in at night, Bruce was exhausted, the boys were starving, and Judy was usually on edge.

THE "WHAT" QUESTION

The human brain is hardwired with the desire to learn or know about things. When triggered, the reflex to problem solve, to reason, and to become curious is activated. "The 'What' Question" exercise is one way to trigger the brain's reflexes to move a person's habitual actions and responses out of a previous behavior pattern and to create or develop a new one effectively.

The basis for "The 'What' Question" exercise is rooted in research and theory that dates back to 1878, when Edward Thorndike made his mark in the field of psychology for his work on what he called "the law of effect." Thorndike stated that "responses that produce a satisfying effect in a particular situation become more likely to occur again in that situation, and responses that produce a discomforting effect become less likely to occur again in that situation."[1]

About thirty years later, the famous Russian physiologist Ivan Pavlov's research focused on, among other things, classic conditioning and involuntary reflexes. During his study with canines, Pavlov called this function of behavior the "What-is-it?" reflex and identified the canines' spontaneous response as a form of curiosity.[2]

B. F. Skinner added to the work of his predecessors, surmising that behavior can be shaped through reward reinforcement. Skinner held to the concept that desired behavioral change is possible with reinforcement through "successive approximation"—that is the process of giving the subject a reward or positive reinforcement for any behavior that closely matches the desired response. These rewards reinforce behavior as a subject's actions get closer and closer to the desired outcome. Eventually, through this successive approximation process, an entirely new behavior pattern can be shaped, and a new habit can be developed.[3]

Many recent studies have also indicated that there is definitely a neurological connection linking human memory to decision-making. This connection gives us the ability to imagine what an experience may look like in the future based upon our past experiences. The human brain, however, is also capable of creating an alternative version to its own past experiences, imagining "what if" scenarios outside of what may or may not have happened in the past.[4-7]

PUTTING "THE 'WHAT' QUESTION" TO WORK

Becoming proficient in the use of "The 'What' Question" strategy leads to a greater capacity to envision a vast number of possible outcomes to any given situation. In a critical moment, when you stop and ask yourself questions such as, *"What should I do in this situation?"* or *"What can I do to solve this problem?"* or *"What would Linda's perspective be on this conflict?,"* you will be able to move beyond ideas solely based on your own perspective and past experiences. As you ask *'what'* questions, you can begin to trigger your brain into a mode of curiosity, rather than confusion, and you can begin to activate your problem-solving reflexes. Over time, this new-found curiosity/problem-solving skill can help you to override other negative impulses that may have set you up for lose-lose relational scenarios in the past.

"What would Connie say if I said _____?" *"What action would Janet take if this happened?"* *"What would Shona do?"* Asking the *'what'* questions in each situation can help you to remain present in the moment and stimulate your brain to solve the problem at hand, rather than just to allow your old behavioral patterns to play out the same conflicts in the same way over and over again. Asking *'what'* questions allows you to look at several possible options—not just

from your own perspective, but also from the perspective of a teacher, counselor, mentor, or coach.

In each scenario, "The 'What' Question" exercise includes the following steps:

1. Practice asking yourself questions that begin with the word, "What."

2. Pair the 'what' question with follow-up action.

3. Make a list of possible 'what' questions. Raise your creativity. Get curious. Think out solutions to the problems you're facing.

4. Start with simple questions. Then become more complex.

WHAT do I do next?

WHAT do I say next?

WHAT is my best next step?

WHAT can I do to move the conversation away from tension?

WHAT can I say or do to stop this argument?

WHAT is it going to take for me to… ?

WHAT if I… ?

The exercise should be practiced repeatedly whenever you find yourself in situations where your thoughts or emotions are scattered. This exercise takes some work. It's not difficult, but it does take disciplined, daily practice. As you become more proficient at remaining present in the moment to ask yourself 'what' questions, your efforts will be noticeable, first of all to you, and secondarily to those in your life. When you feel uncomfortable, confused, or disorientated in a conversation or argument, place an awareness on your growing ability to self-regulate intense situations.

Over time, you will begin experiencing the law of effect in action. As your confidence builds, your belief in yourself and your own ability to change will increase. Each time you practice the skill of stopping and considering 'what' questions, you will be actively reshaping your own behavior through strategic, thought-based reinforcement.

SUCCESS WITH THE WHOLE FAMILY

When Frank and I met a week after he had put this strategy into practice, he shared that he was doing well with asking himself 'what' questions. He explained that near the end of the previous week he had struggled a bit. The Friday before he had a particularly stressful workday, and he was tired. He was able to ask himself some 'what' questions, but he was unfocused and was not getting much internal feedback. He was feeling low that evening, and he said he didn't think he could do much more than eat dinner and go to bed.

Susie and the children had noticed the change immediately. The board games remained put away. There were no playful exchanges, and the TV blared. The family moved to the dinner table as they had before the week of playfulness and quality family time. Everyone took their place at the table without a word. Susie was quite aware that Frank was in a mood again. He didn't even acknowledge her or the children at the table.

But Susie was determined. The silence at the dinner table wouldn't do. She couldn't slide backward into silent, tension-filled dinners and nights with the TV droning loudly to fill a disconnected and unhappy space. As Susie began to dish food onto each person's plate, she began to add a little playfulness. "*What* would you like on your plate first, chicken or rice?" She smiled as she tapped the rice bowl then the chicken dish then the rice bowl again, as she rhythmically repeated, "*What? What? What?*"

Ten-year-old Jack picked up the play right away. All eyes around the table followed as he lifted his arm dramatically in the air. He dropped his hand down, with his elbow pointing way up into the air. He exaggerated a grab of his forehead and said, "Let's see. *What* do I want first? *What?*

What? What?" Then Jack looked up, smiled at his mother, and said matter-of-factly, "I'll take rice first!"

Eight-year-old Lilly jumped in on the fun, *"What* do I want first? *Hmm..."* Putting her little hand across her forehead, *"What? What? What?* Let me think... My brain says chicken!"

"My brain says both!" five-year-old Kyle lifted his plate up with a beaming smile.

Frank was taken aback by the game around the table. Up until then, he hadn't realized that the whole family was watching. They were in it with him, supporting him on his journey of practicing his *'what'* question skills. His dark mood lifted. Frank had begun to laugh out loud and join in the play, "I'm with Kyle. I want both!"

The whole family laughed as Susie kissed Frank on the forehead and filled his plate full.

SAY "NO THANKS," AND WALK AWAY

After Bruce and I met, he started to practice "The 'What' Question" exercise to help slow down his thought process at work and at home, and it was working. His first delivery after lunch Monday was to Mr. Campbell's store on Elm Street. Mr. Campbell was particularly bad about asking Bruce to unload his boxes and move products out into the display cases. Bruce had never been able to turn down his requests before, and this always threw him an hour behind for the day.

But this Monday was different. Bruce went to Campbell's store, unloaded his boxes of soda from the truck to the back door, and he waited. While he waited, he took off the glove on his right hand, placed his hand on his forehead, and thought to himself, *What do I say to this guy?* Immediately the answer came to him: *Unfortunately, Mr. Campbell, I'm on a tight timeline and won't be able to help you today.*

It worked! The first day he practiced the exercise, he knocked almost ninety minutes off of his time in the field. For the first time in a long time, Bruce made it back to the yard that day at five minutes past four o'clock.

Later that night, as the fireworks salesmen droned on at his front steps, Bruce inconspicuously moved his hand to his forehead. He silently asked himself, *What do I say to these guys?* As soon as the question was asked, the answer came, *Say 'no thanks,' and walk away.*

Bruce chuckled to himself as he realized the simple truth of what he needed to do. He verbalized what he thought, "No thanks, man. I've got to go." Bruce walked away and shut the door. He knew Judy would be proud of his restraint. He felt quite successful in the moment and couldn't wait to share his victory with her as he walked into the living room.

MAKE IT A HABIT
ASK THE "WHAT" QUESTION
STEPS FOR SUCCESS

After you have clearly set your intention to put "The 'What' Question" excercise into practice, ready yourself by remaining aware in any moments of tension or stressful conflict.

Different from the other exercises, where you are asked to notice changes in the reactions of others, this exercise is a personal one. Your basic purpose is to begin reshaping your own behavior by using a reinforcing question and successive approximation, rewarding yourself as you are successful.

If others comment on your new behavior in real-life, as Frank's family did, that's great! If they don't catch on, however, don't be discouraged.

Once you're confident with your developing skill, you may want to inform your partner or friends about what you're doing and why you're doing it so that they can begin to help support you in your efforts.

Remember the following steps as you develop this new habit:

1. Practice asking yourself questions that begin with "What."
2. Pair the *'what'* question with a follow-up action.
3. Make a list of possible *'what'* questions. Raise your creativity. Get curious. Seek solutions to the problems.
4. Start with simple questions. Then become more complex.

EXERCISE 1:
ASKING THE "WHAT" QUESTIONS IN YOUR HEAD

To build this new relational skill into your life, start by asking the *'what'* questions in your head.

- As a physical reinforcement, lay the palm of your hand across your forehead and place your thumb on one of your temples and your index or middle finger on your other temple. Make it a comfortable, yet deliberate action.
- Think back to the last difficult conversation you had with your partner or friend. Begin to subvocalize your *'what'* questions in regard to the past event.
- Recreate a picture in your mind or imagine what that difficult conversation might look like in the future if you use a *'what'* question.
- Write down any response that comes to your mind.
- Take the practice exercise a step further.
  - Revisit the same last difficult conversation in your mind, and begin to subvocalize your *'what'* questions in regard to the event.
  - This time add to the *'what'* question the perspective of a teacher, counselor, mentor, or coach.

  What would John do in this situation?

What would Connie Say?

What would Shona think?

What action would Janet take?

What would Steve remark?

What would Linda's take be on this situation?

> Now recreate a picture in your mind, or imagine what that difficult conversation might look like in the future if you used this type of *'what'* question.

> Write down any response that comes to your mind.

EXERCISE 2: APPLY THE TECHNIQUE TO A REAL-LIFE SITUATION

Move from the idea of using the strategy internally to applying the exercise in a real-life scenario. Whether you practice the exercise at home or at work, pay close attention to your successes by writing each one down in a journal.

» Follow the four steps in your mind, but verbalize your responses to the *'what'* questions with the other person involved the conflict.

» Once you have practiced the strategy for a month, evaluate your progress. Go back to your journal and count the number of times you logged a success. (Be sure to think back over the month and try to remember all of the successes you had with the exercise that didn't make it into the log. There will be a few. Take a moment to input all those successes as well.)

» Evaluate your growth.

> Did you find the process easy?

> Did you feel your capacity and proficiency increase?

- Did others notice your behavior patterns changing?

» Champion your success, and share it with those you love.

Chapter 5
YOU ARE MORE IMPORTANT THAN THE PROBLEM

Define Your Relationship Intention and Priority

ONE-SIDED WORKLOAD

"I struggle with quieting my mind when my wife talks. I tend to become critical and judgmental." Adam confessed. "I know how to make her situation better, if she would only take my advice."

Adam went on to share an example that happened the previous week. His wife, Lara, started her new job a few months prior. She was enjoying the challenge after being a homemaker for eight years. Both children were in school all day. This made it easier for Lara to rationalize branching out to put her accounting degree to work at a small deli downtown. Her work schedule was part-time, only four hours a day—five, if you included the commute time. Nevertheless, Lara was enjoying focusing on something other than home and hearth.

Being away from home each morning for five hours took Lara's attention from the daily chores she would have been doing if she were not at work. Laundry was piling up, a layer of dust was building up on every open surface, and meals from the deli replaced the home-cooked delights Adam had enjoyed during the week.

Most distressing to Adam was that he and Lara began to bicker almost every night. Lara would share how she felt a bit guilty leaving the house to go to work. Instead of talking to her about her feelings, he would make a comment about the state of the house or the deli sandwiches for dinner *again*. Lara would react with frustration and stop the conversation. The pair were becoming more and more distant in their relationship. He would stay up and watch a late-night show, while she went to bed at the same time as the children.

"You say that Lara's schedule has changed?" Adam nodded his head, and I continued. "Has your schedule changed at all to adjust to the change?"

Adam thought for a minute. "No. I get up and go to work about the same time every day. Most days after work, I meet my colleagues for happy hour at a nearby pub. I usually get home between six and seven each evening, Monday through Thursday. Fridays I spend a little more time out with the guys before I come home." As if anticipating my thoughts, Adam stared at me for a long time. Then he added. "Lara is really good with me going out after work."

In our meeting that day, I summarized the facts for Adam. "Lara has taken twenty hours of her time each week that would have been devoted to the household, and now she is helping the family in a different way as a part-time breadwinner."

"That's correct," Adam acknowledged.

"The benefits to Lara and the family are two-fold. She is using her skills as an accountant, and she is bringing home a paycheck."

"Yep." Adam wondered where the conversation was going.

"The drawbacks to this change are that Lara is away from the house twenty hours a week, so this means the chores normally taken care of are not getting done—not by Lara, anyway."

"Not to mention her increasingly foul mood whenever we talk," Adam added with an edge of resentment.

"Have you thought about helping Lara out around the house during the week?" I asked.

I could see Adam stiffen in defense, but he refrained from commenting.

When the situation was laid out in such a matter-of-fact way, Adam could see that, as his wife's schedule changed, the circumstances of his relationship had changed. He realized that he could be an equal partner in the solution.

JESSE AND FAITH

Faith was ready to end her twelve-year marriage. She was through! She was learning, growing, and changing. But Jesse wasn't. All he did was go to work, watch TV, stress over everything, and complain. Mostly he would get anxious and complain. Faith and Jesse were far from being on the same page when it came to their relationship.

"He treats me like I'm his mother, not his wife!" Faith cried out in frustration. "I have three kids. I don't need him to be my fourth!"

"What exactly does he do that makes you think he is treating you as if you were his mother?" I asked.

Faith began to share Jesse's painfully sad story of neglect and hardship growing up. Jesse was in and out of foster homes most of his childhood, starting at the age of three. His mother would clean herself up from using drugs and secure a job for a few months. Then she would be back in court requesting her parental rights. Jesse and his two sisters would go back and live with his mother for a while. Things would go along well for a few weeks. Then, his mother would relapse into drug use and lose her job. The children ended up taking care of her until Social Services intervened and took the children to a foster home once again.

By age eleven, Jesse was in the foster care system for good. Few interested adoptive parents wanted to adopt a scared and anxious eleven-year-old boy. No couple wanted to adopt three siblings. His younger sisters were adopted out to separate families, and he was left to fend for himself in a group home. It was years before he was reunited with his sisters. Both sisters were in their early twenties and doing well. Jesse was a welder by trade, so his work was profitable, but he continued to struggle emotionally.

"He wants the house and the children to look immaculate. He wants dinner on the table when he gets home." Faith shook her head. "I work all day and get home the same time he does. We have three boys and live on a ranch. Children are messy! A ranch is dusty and dirty!" She resigned herself to disclosing the hardest thing of all, "He wants to pretend everything is fine."

I handed her a box of tissues as she released herself into a fit of sobs.

After a few moments, Faith took a breath and rallied again. "Jesse really is a good person. He works hard, and he loves his family." Wiping the tears away from her cheeks, she confided, "It's just that he has this idea of what 'family' is supposed to be like, and we don't ever seem to measure up."

"Faith, before you decide to leave your marriage, are you open to trying a strategy with your husband?" I asked.

"I am ready to try anything!"

WHAT ARE YOUR INTENTIONS?

There are several components that make up and define a quality relationship. Because of strained, or lack of communication, Adam and Faith lost clear intentions regarding their role and investment in each of their relationships. The basis of a connected relationship stems from pure intention rooted in caring for the other person. This care is essential. From it, everything else healthfully grows. You must start with care. It is true that maintaining a relationship takes work. However, if you hold the mindset that you care about the other person and the relationship, the work required to maintain any relationship is inviting. It becomes something to look forward to and to be desired.

THE SCIENCE OF ATTACHMENT

Let's explore theories and research that support the idea of healthy attachment in relationships. In psychology, *attachment theory* attempts to explain how secure attachment develops in any relationship. The theory illustrates how healthy attachment helps children and adults survive emotional distress and helps them reestablish hope, optimism, and emotional equanimity.[1]

There is evidence from the work of Bowlby and Ainsworth, that attachment development continues on throughout our lives. Caregiving and reciprocity in a relationship over a lifespan is the basis for Bowlby's reference to attachment development as a "cradle-to-grave phenomenon." According to Bowlby, even adults who are struggling with insecure relationships can develop secure ones, if they become involved with a person who knows how to be caring and reciprocal toward them in a relationship.[2]

Indirect evidence that adult relationships can provide an opportunity for increased attachment development over time is found in the research of Shaver and Hazan.[3] They focused their study on adult romantic-bonds, or pair-bonding, within a relationship. Research following Bowlby's work confirms the idea that adult romantic, pair-bonding relationships have a positive effect on insecure individuals becoming secure over time when they are in a relationship with a securely attached partner.[4]

As for relationships which lack connection, one explanation as to why this occurs is theorized by Robert Firestone, Ph.D. Firestone explores the concept of *fantasy bonding,* which is a theoretical construct that serves to explain the illusion of connection with a mother who may be used by a child to relieve anxiety and emotional pain. Firestone theorizes that a child's *illusion* of connection serves to compensate for maternal rejection, neglect, or deprivation of "love-food" from a mature parent. Later in life, *fantasy bonding* may extend to other relationships where destructive bonds tend to form.

Secondary to the formation of a *fantasy bond* in adulthood, an individual may continue the pattern of idealization of a parent and family. He or she may tend to develop a negative or critical view of self and may develop a victimized orientation to life.[5]

This theory is important as it may help couples understand the unseen barriers they face while attempting to have a healthy relationship. Often, adult relationships develop out of an underlying need to compensate for relationship loss, anxiety, emotional pain, or suffering endured as a child growing up.

The good news is that in adulthood a couple can intentionally create a secure and lasting bond with each other. The process requires evaluating the source and nature of the distressful compensation by exploring feelings, thoughts, and experiences together. United, a couple can creatively come up with solutions that relieve the couple's emotional distance and their individual stress. Increased safety, effort, empathy, and positive reassurance with the process provides commonly desired secure emotional comfort and healthy attachment over time.

Regardless of past negative attachment experience, couples can prepare and nurture a secure relationship. They can do this through a process known as *secure base priming*. This process includes activating positive memories or positive experiences where healthy attachments did exist.[6]

It is theorized that when the brain is ready—or *primed*—to activate positive memories in the form of mental images, feelings, and thoughts of attachment, there is an opportunity for soothing or problem-solving.[7]

Using positive relationship memories of events that include feelings and experiences of love, compassion, care, and kindness can assist with diminishing the feelings and emotions that separate a couple. Such memories can temporarily alter the thought process. The separation between a couple is lessened, and a connection is established, even if only for a moment. Over time, these moments of connectedness strung together to allow for a successful pattern or habit to form. Couples begin to act more often as if they have a secure attachment, as they continually practice the positive-thinking patterns together.

GROWING CLOSER EVERY DAY

I introduced Adam to a relational bonding strategy that I call, "You Are More Important Than the Problem." This strategy is based on the clear intention that your partner and the relationship are more important than any problem the two of you will ever face.

Adam was intrigued. I asked him to consider doing three things.

1. I asked him to set aside some time each day to spend with Lara.

   I recommended ten to fifteen minutes together to be dedicated to focus on each other, putting each other first. He was to listen to her, then she was to listen to him during this protected time. They were asked to keep separate journals. He was to write down what Lara shared, what she needed, and what he might do to assist her that day. Lara was to do the same.

2. At the end of the week, on Friday, he was to arrange for a sitter and take Lara out on a date.

   Besides enjoying each other's time together, they were to bring their journals. I asked them to share their journal entries over dessert, focusing on the positive thoughts, words, and actions enacted in situations where either of them could have let the problem take over.

3. Then I asked them to practice the intention that each of them was more important than the problem for at least a month.

   At the end of the month, I advised them to share with each other their newfound insights and successes.

A month later Adam was excited to share how successful he and Lara were at using the "You Are More Important Than the Problem" strategy.

"At first I didn't think we needed the daily practice. But, boy, was I wrong!" Adam laughed. "Lara was totally on board with trying out the plan."

Adam shared how he had started coming straight home after work instead of heading to the pub. Instead, he and Laura shared a happy hour together folding laundry. He forgot how fun it was to cook a meal with her. They had been laughing and enjoying each other's company again. And the children responded well to the positive mood displayed by their parents.

"I am so much less critical and less judgmental," Adam shared with a measure of humility and also a bit of pride. "We are growing closer each day that we practice the strategy!"

WE ARE GOOD, REALLY GOOD

I shared with Faith that often, adult relationships develop out of an underlying need to compensate for relationship loss. In their case, Jesse's current anxiety and emotional pain were likely due to the suffering he endured at the hand of his mother when he was a child.

I asked Faith to start with a simple strategy and stick with it until she saw success. Faith was given a set of affirmations to state aloud while in bed next to Jesse, right before they fell asleep.

First, Faith was to say to herself:

» I am lovable.

» I am capable.

» I am worthwhile in every way.

» I am always more important than the problem we face.

Then she was to take Jesse's hand and say out loud to him:

» You are lovable.

- » You are capable.

- » You are worthwhile in every way.

- » You are always more important than the problem we face.

The next week Faith came to group session unusually quiet. She had a certain glow about her, an inner peace.

"You look different today, Faith," I said.

"I feel different."

"How did the strategy work for you and Jesse?"

"Perfectly." Faith welled up to where it was hard to speak. Between deep breaths, Faith continued. "Last week I was ready to call it quits on everything—my family, my marriage. Now I can't imagine life without either!"

Faith described what it was like the first night saying the affirmations. Jesse knew right away something was different as she lay on her back reciting in her head: *I am lovable. I am capable. I am worthwhile in every way. I am always more important than the problem we face.*

Jesse lay very still next to her. His body was rigid, flat as a board, and his arms were folded tightly across his chest.

Faith gently pulled his arm loose from the wrap and took his hand in hers. She moved close to him without touching any part of him except for his hand. Staring at the ceiling while she worked up the courage to recite out loud, she began: "You are lovable. You are capable. You are worthwhile in every way. You are always more important than the problem we face."

Jesse's response was unexpected. His hand became extremely sweaty, but he held on tight to hers. His other hand balled into a fist, and he pushed hard into his stomach. He began to sob in a way Faith had never heard before. Jesse curled into Faith and released a childhood of pain into her loving embrace.

They stayed like this for what seemed to be hours. When Jesse calmed down, Faith explained about the strategy and why she felt it was needed. Jesse shared that he, too, felt a distance and didn't know what changes were needed to right things between them. He thought Faith was trying to tell him the marriage was over for her. The last thing Jesse wanted was to lose his family. Most of all he didn't want to lose her.

That week, each and every night, Faith and Jesse affirmed their intention to put their relationship first. They began to explore their thoughts and emotions together. In very short order they creatively came up with solutions that restored safety and reduced stress in their relationship and home.

"The kids are still a muddy mess, and there is dust and dirt everywhere," Faith laughed, "but Jesse and me, we are good, really good."

MAKE IT A HABIT
PRACTICE INTENTION AND PRIORITY
STEPS FOR SUCCESS

To attain secure attachments in a relationship, both parties within the relationship must practice. Both people must exercise their skills regularly to gain greater command over them. The process of creating a more secure attachment requires daily discipline. In other words, train your intent on connecting more deeply with your partner. Compare success with each other regularly.

This practice will enable you both to realize success as a result of your efforts.

EXERCISE 1:
PRACTICE INTENTION AND PRIORITY

One way to practice is to develop a daily, weekly, and monthly plan. Establish with your partner when you will meet each day to put each other first. Every week protect some time to reflect together on your respective daily successes. Each month set aside some time together to review and realize how much change has occurred.

The best way to keep a record of your success is to write it down. Keep a personal journal of your intention to place your partner before any problem.

The plan might look like this.

DAILY PRACTICE

- » Pick the best time of day to have a quiet moment with each other. Take no more than ten or fifteen minutes.

- » In separate journals, each of you should then write how you put your partner first before any problem.

- » Share your journal entry with your partner. Talk through the previous day regarding the successes you experienced in putting each other before any problem that arose.

- » See where you were aligned and where you differed in your awareness and experience. Note the success, and the difference, and decide what you both want to focus on for the next day.

WEEKLY PRACTICE

- » At the end of each week, there will be six ten-minute entries about how you put each other first before any problem.

- » On the seventh day take ten minutes and write about the observations you have made in two areas:

- › The first area is all of the strengths or successes you have observed yourself experiencing over the last six days. Note all the positive thoughts, words, and actions you have enacted in situations where you could have let the problem take over.
- › Then focus on the barriers that presented themselves. Note those thoughts, words, and actions that stopped you from making your partner your priority.
» Share your journal entries with your partner. Set new goals for yourself and each other for the next week.

MONTHLY PRACTICE

» Each month take extra time to look back at the volume of entries. What patterns are observed? Has it been easy to write for an entire month? Did you miss days of writing?
- › What are some of the consistent personal strengths you are aware of that were not so obvious before?
- › Is there a pattern of barriers?

» By setting a common intention to focus your attention on putting each other first, change will naturally occur.
- › What changes have you observed about yourself?
- › What changes have you observed about your partner?

Try practicing this exercise for six months to a year. See what becomes of creating a more secure attachment with your partner.

This is only one form of practice. Seek out the best form of practice for yourself and your partner.

EXERCISE 2:
SET YOUR INTENTIONS TO PUT YOUR RELATIONSHIP FIRST

Here is another deliberate practice that works to secure attachments in adult relationships.

Each morning when you wake, take a moment for intentional habit formation to put your relationship first. The time referred to is that time where you are just waking from a dead sleep but are still not fully awake and ready to get out of bed.

On the night table, under the pillow, taped to the wall, or somewhere close, have the following statements ready:

- » I will accept things as they are in my life.
- » I will respect relationship boundaries.
- » I will focus on my/our small successes.
- » I will forgive myself and my partner.
- » I will put love first—always and in every situation.
- » I will put myself and my partner before any problem that we face.

At the end of each day, when you are in bed, just as you turn out the light, continue the intentional habit formation.

Let the following statements be the last thing you and your partner think of and say before you doze off to sleep.

Say to yourself:

- » I am lovable.
- » I am capable.
- » I am worthwhile in every way.
- » I am always more important than the problem that we face.

Then say to your partner:

- » You are lovable.
- » You are capable.
- » You are worthwhile in every way.
- » You are always more important than the problem that we face.

Chapter 6
CLARIFY BOUNDARIES

Un-Muddle the Jumble

NOT-SO PEACEFUL CONTACT

Madeline found it hard to speak. She came to group session sobbing, and fifteen minutes in she was still crying.

"Are you okay, Madeline?" I went on, "Are you safe right now?" I wanted to be sure she was out of harm's way.

"He just won't stop." More sobbing, "He thinks he still lives here, and he doesn't." Madeline blew her nose loudly. "He comes in, picks up my phone, and scrolls through my messages. He sits at the computer and tries to figure out my password. He goes into the bedroom to see if anyone is there—or has been there. He just acts like he can come in anytime he wants! I'm sick of it!"

"How does he get in?" I wondered out loud.

"The kids will let him in, or he comes in through the back door." Madeline shared that she had enough money to change the locks on the front door but not enough to replace them on the back door.

Madeline told the group about the *'peaceful contact'* order that was in place. "He is allowed to contact me as long as all contact is peaceful." She wiped away the tears from her eyes. Then she began listing things on her fingers, "He can't hit, grab, throw things, swear at me, or damage my property." In frustration, she said, "The order doesn't say anything about walking through a door or looking at my phone or computer!"

"But a peaceful contact order does include not disturbing your peace by arguing. He is not supposed to argue with you, right?" I pressed on, "He is also not to do anything that makes you frightened, upset, or disturbed. Isn't that right?"

Madeline nodded and listened.

"Do you say anything to your ex-husband when he walks in the house uninvited and starts upsetting you with his intrusive behaviors?"

"No." Madeline looked down at the tissue wadded up in her hand. "I promised myself I wouldn't create a scene in front of the children." She paused then went on. "Last time I tried to stand up for myself he got abusive and threatened me."

"Bring your contact order next session, so we can review it," I said.

Madeline agreed she would bring the papers the next time we met.

FAMILY REUNION

Craig hated going to his wife's Fourth of July family reunion. He had been to five previous gatherings, and this year would make six. His wife had two brothers and three male cousins who really didn't like him at all. As soon as Craig and his wife arrived, the hurtful comments would begin. One by one a brother-in-law or cousin would pass by Craig and say something to antagonize him.

"Got a job yet?"

"Better not be laying a hand on my sister."

"Dead-beat dad."

About halfway through the reunion, the family bullies would come at him in pairs or trios. After each taunting insult, the laughter would follow. Craig's wife was aware of what was going on, but she didn't know what to say or do to make it stop. At a couple of the previous events, Craig had gotten so upset that he started a fight with one or more of them. Even when a row didn't ensue, for five years running, Craig and his wife left the event early with their children. The family never stayed long enough to watch the fireworks. Craig's wife would get upset, and Craig felt bruised, battered, and angry. He just wanted the bullying to stop.

WHAT IS A BOUNDARY?

Madeline and Craig struggled with setting boundaries. A boundary is a line set to create a real or unseen border or divide between people, places, ideas, or things. Madeline struggled with establishing a clear boundary with her ex-husband. Similarly, Craig did not know how to go about setting a boundary with his wife's male family members.

When we think of common boundaries, we think of lines and borders established between countries, states, cities, and individual property lines. Boundaries such as these are based on geography, political governance, or perhaps historical divides. Governing bodies come together, and, based on established rules of law, decide what to do if a city grows past its borders or if a neighbor encroaches a property line by putting up a new fence that extends onto your lawn.

When thinking of setting personal boundaries, the formation rules are less clear. But they don't have to be jumbled or clouded. Any boundary that is present may exist as a result of happenstance rather than explicit decision making or planning on the part of an individual.

Familial and relational boundaries can be unclear simply because of the parties' physical proximity to each other. You live in each other's most intimate spiritual, mental, emotional, and physical spaces.

Then, too, some people have a natural tendency to overstate or understate a boundary. When a boundary is crossed, it may be forgiven readily, or, conversely, it may be unreasonably reinforced. This mixed messaging makes for real confusion on boundary clarity over time. One day you see that your teenage daughter has borrowed your favorite shirt, and you say nothing. On another day a yelling match ensues when she asks to borrow the shirt again.

In the article, "What Do You Mean 'Boundaries'?" Dr. Henry Cloud and Dr. John Townsend write:

> *Boundaries define us. They define what is me and what is not me. A boundary shows me where I end and someone else begins, leading me to a sense of ownership. Knowing what I am to own and take responsibility for gives me freedom.*[1,2]

Marvin G. Knittel, Ed.D, describes three types of personal boundaries. He defines these types in this way:

1. Someone with healthy boundaries is someone who is able to value his or her own opinion, is not willing to compromise individual values for other people, appropriately shares personal information, and is accepting of others when they say "no" to them.

2. Someone with rigid boundaries tends to avoid intimacy and close relationships, usually doesn't ask for help, has few close relationships, may seem detached, and distances him- or herself to prevent rejection.

3. The third type described is a person with porous boundaries. This is someone who tends to over-share personal information, has difficulty saying no to the requests of others, gets over-involved with other's problems, and tolerates abuse or disrespect.[3]

Allison Bottke, in **Setting Boundaries with Negative Thoughts and Painful Memories,** holds that boundaries help one maintain sanity. She describes the goal of sanity as to help protect and nurture our hearts—the center of all the vital activities of body, soul, and spirit; of our personality, and of our character. Too, she writes, healthy boundaries do not develop in a vacuum or in isolation.[4,5]

We are not separate from others or the world around us. For the purposes of this work, our focus is on helping individuals develop healthy boundaries within a relational environment. If we can set healthy boundaries with others, places, and things, we are more able to avoid stiffening into rigid and detached ways of interacting in our relationships, and there is less likelihood of our healthy boundaries being penetrated or crossed.

BOUNDARY FIRMLY IN PLACE

Madeline was upbeat when she came to the group session. She couldn't wait to share her new understanding of the "peaceful contact" provision in the court order.

"It says here..." Madeline started in when she was called to share. "The peaceful contact provision permits the abuser—that's him—to peacefully communicate with the victim—that's me—for limited reasons, including the care and transfer for visitation of their child." She looked up to emphasize the *'limited reasons'* part. "It also says he is not to annoy or disturb my peace!" She dropped the paper in her lap and proclaimed, "His behavior is beyond reason! And, he certainly is annoying and disturbing me!"

The group members began to laugh. They could see Madeline coming to life before them. Her new-found understanding of the order was not new to the other participants. They had been there, done that, and were all supportive. Not all of them had a restraining or protective order in their history; however, all of them did struggle with setting and keeping boundaries in their relationships. One by one they shared the moment when they realized it was they who needed to not only set the boundaries in their relationships, but that they also needed to be the ones to take responsibility for enforcing those boundaries. The group talked about how they accomplished healthy boundary setting in their relationships. Together we offered viable suggestions to Madeline to help with her situation.

By the next group session, Madeline had taken action. Everyone in the group wanted to hear about her progress. Madeline shared that she went to the court and petitioned to amend the order. Her petition was granted. She asked for a *'stay away provision,'* ordering her ex-husband to stay at least one hundred yards away from her home and car. She also requested and received a counseling provision ordering her ex-husband to attend counseling. Her rationale was that she wanted their children to see their father. She just wanted the children to be safe in his presence.

Madeline laughed and then sighed. "I looked out the window two nights ago to find my ex sitting on the curb across from the house, hunched over, with his head hanging low. He looked so sad and pitiful." She sobered. "He is the father of my children. I hope one day we can be civil with one another. But, for now, I've made sure the boundary is firmly in place!"

WATCHING THE FIREWORKS

Craig was determined that he was not going to fight at this year's family reunion. He and his family were going to stay until the end and enjoy the fireworks. After our counseling session, he decided to practice setting a boundary to reject conflict by imagining a physical wall between himself and his wife's relatives. Craig went home from our meeting, shared his intentions with his wife, and explained the strategy. Both Craig and his wife were optimistic about having a plan to deal with the bullying they knew would come.

On the Fourth of July, Craig and his family arrived early to the event and set up their picnic table under a large oak tree. Within the first fifteen minutes, right on cue, Craig's wife's older brother came over and made a snide remark. Craig was ready. He put his strategy into practice. He imagined a physical boundary wall being placed between himself and his brother-in-law. Then Craig imagined the negative comments of his brother-in-law hitting and then bouncing right off of that imaginary wall. They could not get through. A smile crossed Craig's face as the strategy worked to calm him.

Craig cheerfully replied to the cruel comment, "Hey brother! Happy Fourth of July!"

Craig's brother-in-law hesitated for a moment and then walked past a little perplexed at the positive response.

A few minutes later, one of the cousins walked by and said something off color. Craig was not only ready, but he had a bit more confidence after the first outcome. Again, he imagined a boundary wall between himself and the cousin. And this time, Craig laughed out loud. He turned away from the cousin and toward his wife who was smiling broadly. They reached across the table to hold each other's hands as the cousin walked on by.

Awhile later, another cousin happened by. Before the bully said a word, Craig looked the cousin straight in the eye and said, "Hey man. Can we not do this again? I really want to stay and let my family watch the fireworks."

The cousin hesitated for a minute. Then he rounded the picnic table and sat down next to Craig's wife. She offered him some food, and the three of them just sat for a moment wondering why they hadn't broken the cycle years ago.

For the first time in six years, Craig and his family were able to stay and watch the fireworks without incident. On the ride home, Craig felt closer to his wife than he had in years. He felt his confidence rise as he replayed the events of the day. He remarked later that the success was small and quiet, but it was a success nonetheless.

MAKE IT A HABIT
CLARIFYING BOUNDARIES
STEPS FOR SUCCESS

One way to approach boundary setting for self is to think in terms of four areas: spiritual, mental, emotional, and physical.

EXERCISE 1 EXAMPLE: WRITE DOWN YOUR BOUNDARIES

Using the lined area at the end of the exercises, write down three boundaries that are effectively in place for you in each of the four areas listed below.

For example:

- Spiritual
  - I set aside protected time each day to pray or meditate.
  - I read spiritual literature a few times a week.
  - I attend my place of worship once a week.
- Mental
  - I read for pleasure every night before going to bed.
  - I leave thoughts and responsibilities related to work at work.
  - I avoid negative thinking and conversations.
- Emotional
  - I ensure that I have time alone for myself and make self-care a priority each day.
  - I am responsible for my thoughts and feelings and expressing them.
  - I am clear with my family members about what I believe, want, and need.
- Physical
  - I eat healthy each day.
  - I work out at least four times a week.

> I spend weekends outdoors walking, hiking, kayaking, swimming, biking, skiing, etc.

EXERCISE 2 EXAMPLE: NOTE AREAS WHICH NEED IMPROVED BOUNDARIES

Look at the information you wrote down for Exercise 1. Be honest with yourself, and note which areas listed have solid boundaries and which have a bit of waiver each week. Indicate one example in each area where a boundary can be strengthened.

For example:

» Spiritual

> While I would like to read spiritual literature a few times a week, there are times when weeks will go by where I don't pick up a spiritual book at all.

» Mental

> I don't always leave thoughts and responsibilities related to work at work. There are times when I cross my own boundary and think of a work problem all night. I might even bring work home to complete that I was unable to finish in the day.

» Emotional

> I am not always clear with my family members about what I believe, want, and need.

» Physical

> I really intend to eat healthy each day, but during the holidays there are always homemade treats in the breakroom at work. I find myself slipping into the room to nibble on cookies, candy, and pie.

EXERCISE 3 EXAMPLE:
MAKE A CHOICE ABOUT YOUR BOUNDARIES

Look at the information you wrote in Exercise 2. Make a choice to firm up the boundary or grace yourself and let the boundary go.

For example:

» Spiritual

› I want to reestablish the goal of reading spiritual literature a few times a week. I will set this boundary for myself by placing the spiritual literature next to my pleasure reading on my nightstand. That way, I will be reminded to read from both books before going to sleep.

» Mental

› I want to amend the boundary around leaving thoughts and responsibilities related to work at work. The truth is there is too much work for me to finish in the workday. I will set a firm boundary to bring work home to complete that I was unable to finish in the day only one day a week on Thursdays. That way, any additional work that piles up between Monday and Thursday will be taken care of Thursday night after dinner.

» Emotional

› I need to be more explicit with my boundaries around communicating with my family members about what I believe, want, and need. First, I will make an effort to assess what I believe, want, and need each day. Then I will set aside protected time to discuss those issues with my spouse/partner.

» Physical

› I am going to give myself a break around the holidays. I eat healthy most days. I will allow myself one homemade treat from the breakroom at work during the holidays.

EXERCISE 4 EXAMPLE: CONSIDER THE THOUGHTS, FEELINGS, AND ACTIONS OF OTHERS

Assess if the thoughts, feelings, and actions or others infringe upon or cross any of your established boundaries. If they do, clearly set the boundary for everyone concerned.

For example:

» Spiritual

> I set aside protected time each day to pray. My spouse/partner and children walk in and out of the room where I pray.

☐ *I will have a family meeting to talk about the need for protected, quiet space for praying.*

☐ *I will place a 'Quiet Please, In Prayer' sign on the door of the room*

☐ *I will speak to the individual if the boundary is mistakenly crossed thereafter.*

» Mental

> I avoid negative thinking and conversations. Every time a co-worker engages me in the breakroom, she begins talking negatively about the boss.

☐ *I will take time to speak to the coworker privately and let her know that I am not comfortable talking negatively about the boss.*

☐ *I will tell her that, if she tries to engage me in such conversation, I will let her know then and there that I am uncomfortable before walking out of the room.*

- ☐ *I will recommend that she take up her concerns directly with the boss.*

» Emotional

> I am responsible for my thoughts and feelings and expressing them. My teenage daughter runs in the kitchen, opens the refrigerator door, and complains about not having anything good to eat. She stomps to her room, slams the door, and refuses to come out.

- ☐ *In a quiet moment, I will take the time to sit with my daughter to discuss the inappropriateness of her actions and about her taking responsibility for her behavior.*
- ☐ *I will reinforce my availability to her to share her beliefs, thoughts, and feelings.*
- ☐ *I will model appropriate behavior for her by sharing my beliefs, thoughts, and feelings.*

» Physical

> I spend weekends outdoors walking, hiking, kayaking, swimming, biking, skiing, etc. My spouse/partner expects the garage to be cleaned out at the same time I have arranged for outdoor time.

- ☐ *I will sit with my spouse/partner and remind him/her of my prior engagement.*
- ☐ *I will support his/her desire to clean the garage and set up an alternative time for us to get the job done together.*

Once you are able to practice setting clear boundaries for yourself, setting boundaries with others becomes second nature. Bounce the beliefs, wants, and needs of others off of what you know you believe, need, and want. You will find comfort in being able to assess if someone is crossing a boundary with you or not. Those who care about you will be clear that you pray every day and go to your place of worship each week. They will understand that you walk away from conversations where there is negative thinking or discussion. They will support you in needing time alone and in knowing that self-care is a priority. And, perhaps they will join you on your outdoor adventures on the weekend.

EXERCISE 1:
WRITE DOWN THREE BOUNDARIES THAT ARE EFFECTIVELY IN PLACE FOR YOU IN THE FOUR AREAS

- » Spiritual
    - › _____
    - › _____
    - › _____

- » Mental
    - › _____
    - › _____
    - › _____

- » Emotional
    - › _____
    - › _____
    - › _____

- » Physical
    - › _____
    - › _____
    - › _____

EXERCISE 2:
NOTE AREAS WHERE YOUR BOUNDARIES CAN BE STRENGTHENED

- » Spiritual
    - › _____

- » Mental
    - › _____

- » Emotional
    - › _____

- » Physical
    - › _____

EXERCISE 3:
CHOOSE TO FIRM UP THE BOUNDARY OR TO GRACE YOURSELF AND LET THE BOUNDARY GO

- » Spiritual
    - › _____

» Mental

　› _____

» Emotional

　› _____

» Physical

　› _____

EXERCISE 4: CONSIDER THE THOUGHTS, FEELINGS, AND ACTIONS OF OTHERS

» Spiritual

　› My boundary is_____.

　› The infringement on this boundary is:

　_____

　› I will _____

- > I will _____

- > I will _____

- » Mental
  - > My boundary is_____.
  - > The infringement on this boundary is:

  - > I will _____

  - > I will _____

  - > I will _____

CLARIFY BOUNDARIES

- Emotional
  - My boundary is_____.
  - The infringement on this boundary is:

    _____

    _____

    _____

  - I will _____

    _____

    _____

  - I will _____

    _____

    _____

  - I will _____

    _____

    _____

- Physical
  - My boundary is_____.
  - The infringement on this boundary is:

    _____

    _____

    _____

  - I will _____

    _____

    _____

› I will _____

_____

_____

› I will _____

_____

_____

Chapter 7
MOTIVATION

Find One Strong Reason to Act

FIRST STEPS

James struggled with depression and a lack of motivation for more than half a year. This wasn't always the case. He had goals, ambition, and a desire for life that others envied. In the middle of this time of depression, James came to see me. He shared that, as of late, he found himself stuck in a fog of indecisiveness about most things in his life. James knew his attitude and behavior had put his marriage on the rocks.

Janet, James's wife of five years, still loved him, but she couldn't take the attitude, bad behavior, or abuse any longer. She had left him six months prior to our first meeting and filed formal separation papers in court. As Janet slipped away, she took their two kids to her mother's house and added to the court documents by filing a restraining order against James.

By court order, James was not allowed to contact Janet or the children, and he was not to come within one hundred and fifty feet of the family he loved.

All this had taken a tremendous toll on James. When he came to my office, he explained that he barely recognized the man he used to be. Of course, he understood why Janet took such drastic actions to leave. His cruelty to her at the bitter end had surprised even him. Nonetheless, James claimed that he still missed his wife and the children desperately.

As I spoke with James, he shared that the time spent on his legal battles had taken a toll on his career, as well. A few months into the ordeal, James was fired from his position after four years of loyal service at his company. His friends and family stopped calling. James felt utterly alone with absolutely no support.

I could see that James had fallen into a deep bout of clinical depression. The signs were obvious. He found himself lacking the basic motivation for self-care. His hair was growing long and unkempt. He went unshaven for days, and he told me that he honestly couldn't remember the last time he had taken a shower. James, who previously was a gregarious individual, life-of-the-party kind of guy, found himself becoming increasingly reclusive, simply sleeping away each day.

"So, what prompted you to call me?" I asked James in our first appointment together.

James began to recount his story. Just before he contacted my office, James said he had gotten a phone call from his mother-in-law. It was unusual for her to call him even under normal circumstances, and he hadn't spoken to her at all since Janet had left him six months ago. His mother-in-law said she was contacting him because Janet couldn't call due to the restraining order that was in place. She said Janet wanted to let him know that their one-year-old daughter had taken her first step.

With the news, James dropped the cell phone to his heart. As he told me what happened, his eyes welled with emotion, and he began to cry. He took a moment to compose himself, and then he went on with his story.

While still holding the phone, he heard his mother-in-law's voice. "James, are you still there? James?" She became quiet for a long while as she listened and held the space for her son-in-law to grieve. "James, listen to me. Are you listening?"

James took a deep breath and exhaled loudly. He placed the phone to his ear. "Yes, I'm here."

"Do you remember your vows to my daughter, James? Do you remember what you committed to her on your wedding day?"

"No man without woman, no woman without man, neither without God." James recited his vows without hesitation, as though he had said those words just yesterday.

"Do you think you're upholding those vows today James?" She asked in a soft but firm tone.

James was silent.

She went on, "Janet filed separation papers, not divorce papers. She loves you, James. She wants her family back. But you have a lot of work to do on your end before she's willing to reconcile. Your attitude, your behavior, your cruelty, it all must stop. Are you motivated to keep your family together, James? Are you willing to do the work it will take to reunite your family?"

James's grief opened into uncontrollable sobs on the phone. Between tears and gasps for air James unleashed his fear, "I don't know what to do. What do I do? I miss Janet and the kids so much! I need help!"

His mother-in-law once again held the space open for him to release his pent-up emotions. "The first step is recognizing you have a problem and need help, James. And you have just taken that first step."

REDUCED TO REPETITION

Stan came to the group session frustrated and unhappy. His motivation at work had significantly decreased over the last month. Stan was a biochemist working as a laboratory scientist, and the lab was working on a special project. He and two other scientists were hand-picked to do the work.

Initially, Stan was excited about his new assignment. Initially—because, for three months running Stan was tasked with recreating the same chemical reaction process over and over again all day, every day. The repetition was grating on Stan's nerves. Nothing new ever happened. For ninety days, everything had been the same, and the worst part was that the assignment was supposed to last for another three long months.

Stan couldn't take it anymore, and his lack of motivation was causing him to make mistakes. He was spending more and more of his time correcting his errors instead of accurately recreating the required reaction process. Stan's attitude started to sour. He began coming in late to work, and each day, he skipped out at least fifteen to twenty minutes early, leaving the other two members of the select team holding the bag.

It was only a matter of time before the head researcher on the project, Dr. Moore, noticed the decrease in Stan's performance. In the project's controlled environment all errors and restarts of the process were carefully logged. Stan's errors were increasing daily each week.

Dr. Moore had hand-picked Stan for the project. She was confident in his educational background, experience, and specialized skills as a biochemist. But over the last three months, she had learned about Stan's motivation—or lack thereof. Stan was losing his ability to attend to the tasks asked of him. She saw that he lacked the big-picture perspective of the critical work in front of him. His avoidant behaviors with the people on his team, with her, and with the requirements of the task were of great concern.

The day before our group session, Dr. Moore had called Stan into her office to discuss his lack of motivation. "Stan, you know you were hand-picked for this assignment. At the beginning of the project, you were all in, excited, really motivated to be a part of this team. Lately, I see your errors are up. You are coming in late and leaving early. What's going on?"

Stan hung his head low.

THIS THING CALLED MOTIVATION

Motivation is an interesting concept. It's defined as the sense of need or desire that prompts an individual to act. In the stories above, both James and Stan lost motivation in their lives.

Theorists have studied the theory of motivation for years. What motivates a person to get up early in the morning while another is motivated to remain in bed until almost noon? What pushes an athlete to work out three hours a day, six days a week while someone else is content to walk around the block on Sunday?

TYPES OF MOTIVATION

Is motivation innate or is it affected by the environment; or both?

One view is that motivation is a driving force—something that activates us through sheer physical or mental power. The key idea behind motivation being a driving force is largely that it is a "mechanical" behavior. An example of this could be seen in someone who, without prompting, is disciplined about getting up every morning at five o'clock for a mile swim. Some force within them simply compels them to do it.

Another view is that motivation stems from arousal, a sense of excitement or stirring up. The motivation, in this case, depends upon the level of excitement one experiences. If the individual is not stirred up, they are not motivated to act. A mountain climber, seeing a picture of a steep cliff is motivated to climb because they are aroused by the image.

From a cognitive view, motivation is carried along by an intrinsic force. Something inherent or essential prompts it. Those who are motivated through intrinsic force experience a measure of self-reward in their endeavors. They are moved to feel competent or capable. An example of this type of intrinsic-force motivation might be someone who works on a creative project, finding reward in the process, as well as, in the final product.

In some, receiving attention from others and one's surroundings is a strong motivator. Many people are motivated by public recognition or reward.

Conversely, avoidance of others or surroundings can also be a motivator. Someone avoiding thoughts, feelings, and negative actions is motivated to move away from external influences. For example, someone who does not want to discuss a sensitive issue will avoid it by shutting the other person off or walking away.

Finally, seeking self-actualization is a motivator. The technical terms for these words give us an understanding of this type of motivation. *Self* means *the individuality or nature of someone*. *Actualization* means *the act of existing as fact, as opposed to potential*. Together, *self-actualization* means *the factual aspect of someone's individuality or nature*. A person motivated to be self-actualized has a learned need for fulfillment. Going back to Maslow's hierarchy, those who seek motivation through self-actualization move through a hierarchy of needs to be complete. They strive for fundamental needs such as being safe, belonging, understanding, and loving.

So is motivation innate or is it merely a reaction to a person's environment? It can be argued that all the types of motivations discussed have both inherent and environmental factors at work.

THE SCIENCE BEHIND MOTIVATION

In 1977, Albert Bandura presented a theoretical framework to explain and predict psychological changes achieved by different motivating factors. Bandura wanted to explore motivation from the context of studying expected outcomes concerning coping skills and behaviors. Basically, he wanted to observe how long subjects would continue their coping efforts in the face of adversity.

The results of his research indicated that there is a strong correlation between perceived self-efficacy and behavioral change. In layman's terms, if the subject felt they could be successful, they remained motivated in the face of adversity; however, if a subject's belief in their ability to produce a desired result began to wane, their motivation faded right along with it.[1]

An Associate professor at the University of Reading, and head of the Motivation Science Lab, Kou Murayama, conducted some interesting research on the connection between motivation and memory. His study in 2011 indicated that there was a difference between performance-approach goals and mastery-approach goals. His findings suggested that an investment in performance wins over the result of eventual mastery.[2]

In other words, he theorized that motivation is more about how one applies themselves to the *process* of any task. The *outcome* of the process seems to be less of a driving force. A painter paints because the process of painting is motivating. The end result, a finished painting, whether deemed good or bad, is less of a motivator. The painter is motivated to pull out a new canvas and begin painting once again.

In a study of the effects of motivation on learning, Carol Dweck observed the adaptive and maladaptive motivational patterns of children. Her findings indicated that motivational patterns, without a concerted effort to the contrary, stayed with an individual throughout adulthood. Dweck postulated that motivational processes developed early in a child's life shaped their reactions to success and failure and influenced the quality of their cognitive performance throughout their lives.[3] Specifically, as a child's motivational processes were identified, it seems that those same motivating factors were the factors that compelled them into the future. Their motivation affected their learning skills.

PUTTING "THE MOTIVATION STRATEGY" TO WORK: A PERSONAL ASSESSMENT

It's important that we do a personal assessment of our motivational type, or types, to determine how to employ this strategy in bringing about a change in our relational patterns. To do a personal assessment simply means that we must determine through investigation, the value or worth, of a particular motivational stimulus to effect a change in ourselves. In other words, what works best for you?

How are you motivated? Consider the sense of need, desire, or compulsion that prompts you to act in general, then more specifically, think in terms of how you are motivated with aspects of layered emotion and feeling. Think about your environmental factors as well. Assess which types of motivation fit for you.

Are you motivated by driving force, arousal, cognitive or intrinsic motivations? Do you feel motivated as a means of getting attention, a means to avoid something or someone, or are you striving for self-actualization?

The following text is written in the first person to assist you in the exploration of understanding your own personal motivation more fully. It is written as though it pertains to you.

At the end of each section, there are two statements. Assess which of the two statements apply to you.

DRIVING FORCE

I tend to activate physically or with mental force when I am emotional. A primary function behind driving force is to reestablish balance in the moment. *Balance* means *to remain in equilibrium.* I do not like whatever is going on, so I seek a sense of balance.

As mentioned previously, an internal driving force is primarily a mechanical behavior. It's as if your behavior is performed by some inner machinery, thus driving-force motivators are balanced and mechanical. I identify my thoughts, emotions, and behavior as being mechanically driven.

☐　I am motivated by driving force.

☐　I am not motivated by driving force.

AROUSAL

I tend to get excited or stirred up easily. My thoughts, emotions, and behavior are based on the level of excitement I experience. *Excitement* means *to arouse intensely.* If there is no excitement associated with my thoughts, emotions, and or behavior, then I am not stirred up and am not motivated to act. I identify my thoughts, emotions, and behavior as being based on arousal.

- ☐ I am motivated by arousal.
- ☐ I am not motivated by arousal.

INTRINSIC

My emotions and behaviors are motivated by inherent or essential thoughts. *Inherent* means *a permanent characteristic or quality.* They are essential, such that I cannot do without these motivators. I am compelled through these intrinsic forces because I get a measure of self-reward. I feel competent when my thoughts are realized through my emotions and behaviors.

- ☐ I am intrinsically motivated.
- ☐ I am not intrinsically motivated.

ATTENTION

My thoughts, emotions, and behaviors are motivated by the attention I receive from others around me. My surroundings play a significant role in how I think, feel, and behave. I am moved by the reward of external reflection and response. I look for external praise and reward.

- ☐ I am motivated by attention.
- ☐ I am not motivated by attention.

AVOIDANCE

I avoid people, conversations, and most of all confrontations. Most often I want to get out of the way of others or remove myself from particular surroundings. I do not like to discuss sensitive issues, even in my most trusted relationships. I say little, shut others out, and/or walk away from situations where I feel uncomfortable.

- ☐ I am motivated by avoidance.
- ☐ I am not motivated by avoidance.

SELF-ACTUALIZATION

Thinking, feeling, and behaving is in my nature. All aspects of my nature teach me about myself and about life. How I think, feel, and behave assists me in striving to attain my fundamental needs such as being safe, belonging, understanding, and loving. If I can successfully acknowledge and accept my thoughts, feelings, and behaviors, the closer I will be to being complete.

- ☐ I am motivated by self-actualization.
- ☐ I am not motivated by self-actualization.

This mini motivation assessment is designed to offer insight into how you uniquely motivate yourself. You may find that you have two or three different sources for your motivation. There may be times when thoughts activate your motivation. At other times you may be motivated by emotion or behavior.

It's important to note that there are no right or wrong answers. There are no good or bad motivational factors. The exercise serves merely to inform and help you become aware of your unique motivating factors. Then, if motivated, you can intentionally work to develop the type, or types, of motivation you don't identify with but may prefer.

PEACEFUL CONTACT

As James sat in my office detailing the reasons he was motivated to seek my assistance, I listened to the rest of his story.

James said he sat for a long while after the call with his mother-in-law ended. Something shifted in his mind that stemmed from a shift in his heart. He felt an urgent sense of desire to see his family. He needed to get out of the house and find some help in getting his family back. James was prompted to act. He picked up his cell phone and searched for marriage therapists near him. He found a therapist with five satisfaction stars from an Internet referral network, and he made an appointment for the following day.

Janet deserved his best, and he wanted her to know of his efforts. James called his mother-in-law back. He thanked her for reaching out to him with the news of his daughter's first steps. More importantly, he thanked her for her challenging words. He wanted her to know her call had motivated him to seek help, and he had scheduled an appointment to see a marriage therapist the next day. James also asked his mother-in-law if he could make weekly calls to her merely to check in on his family and share his progress.

Once James completed his first therapy session, there was no stopping him. His driving force became winning Janet's heart back, making amends, and reuniting his family. James went on to get a job doing the same type of work as he had done before, but he was actually making more money per hour at his new place of employment. On the advice of his therapist, James took an anger management and parenting course. He also connected up with me for additional counseling.

Although he still wasn't able to see his family, James started a photo journal for his children. Every day he would write a letter to each of them. He also took pictures of himself in places where he wanted to take them eventually. James had been making weekly calls to his mother-in-law telling her all about his progress. She would update him on the children and how Janet was fairing throughout the separation. Reuniting with his family was all he could think about.

Three months into James's efforts he shared with me that he had received an official letter in the mail. It was from the court. He opened the envelope with a measure of dread. He had been working so hard. Were these divorce papers? He felt a swell of emotion as he unfolded the document.

The words jumped off the page, *"The restraining order has been amended to a Peaceful Contact Order..."* James couldn't focus on any other part of the document. Was it true? Could he really go and visit his family? He picked up the phone and dialed his mother-in-law immediately.

"The restraining order has been amended to 'peaceful contact.' Did you know? Is it true?" James blurted out finding it hard to contain his excitement.

"Yes, James," His mother-in-law replied. "Janet went to the court and had the order amended."

Then James made a humble request: "Could I speak to Janet, please?" Tears streamed down his face as he waited for a reply.

"James?" Janet asked through her own tears.

"I am so sorry, ...so very sorry, sweetheart." James kept repeating himself between sobs. "Would it be okay if I came over to visit you and the kids today?" he asked.

"Please. And stay for dinner. Mom and dad will be going out for a few hours. We will have the house to ourselves. I'll make your favorite."

James's sobs were uncontrollable.

Still crying, Janet said, "Thank you, James. Thank you for caring enough about our family to change. We'll still need more time to work things out, but we can talk later. For now, let's start by you getting over here to see your daughter walk."

MOTIVATED BY VALUE AND PURPOSE

Stan told the support group what happened next. As he spoke to his supervisor, Dr. Moore, he clasped his hands together and slid down into the chair. He was as direct with her as she was with him. "I don't really know what's going on. I have been alone with my thoughts in that sterile room, all day, every day, for three months now." Stan sighed, "The other chemists and I don't interact at all. I'm not even inclined to discuss work with them at break, because I know what they are going through, too. They're busy doing exactly what I do. I don't really know them all that well, so I don't have anything else to talk to them about."

Dr. Moore looked up, "Well, I didn't expect to do a secondary research study while working on this special project, but it looks like I will have to incorporate a small study into the mix, nevertheless. I am adding to your duties, Stan."

Stan pushed himself up in the chair and looked at Dr. Moore with more curiosity than he had felt all month. "Oh, really?"

"Yes," Dr. Moore replied. "You will be leading the team in a query-based discussion each morning before starting on your daily work. I'll place a specific control question about the project on the whiteboard. I want you to help the team dissect the question for full understanding. Then I want you and the team to ponder the possible answers to the question throughout the day while you conduct your reaction processes. And during the last thirty minutes of each day, you will lead the others through an exercise of writing down the various answers from your team. Write everything down, and leave your work on my desk."

Stan was excited by the prospects of this new task. Each morning he would collaborate and brainstorm with his colleagues regarding one question. At the break, he would meet up with the team over coffee or tea to discuss the thoughts they had throughout the morning specifically relating to that day's question. At the end of each day, all three scientists scribbled their multiple answers onto sheets of paper, as they pondered the possibilities. Stan dropped their work onto Dr. Moore's desk every day before leaving for home.

After a month, Dr. Moore called Stan into her office. Two charts covered the wall behind her as she sat at the desk. Dr. Moore explained, "Over here on this graph you can see the twenty questions given to you and team." Dr. Moore pointed to the chart on the left. "You and the team have assisted me in dealing with the major questions I have been struggling with since the project began."

Stan rose and moved to the chart. He could see the answers he and the team came up with neatly categorized into columns of priority on the graph. A smile spread over his face as he finally visualized the team's efforts over the last month.

Dr. Moore moved her hand back to a section of the chart on the right. "Stan, this is your personal productivity chart for the last month."

Stan crossed in front of the chart and his smile broadened. "Wow!"

"Wow is right, Stan. The errors in your work have decreased significantly to the expected one to two a day. Look." Dr. Moore pointed to small section on the graph from the previous week. "You were error free on these three consecutive days." Dr. Moore paused to allow Stan to take in her words. "You were on time to work for the last twenty days, and you've been leaving ten to fifteen minutes after five o'clock."

Stan knew he was doing better, but not that much better. "I guess your research worked! I have been more motivated. Tackling a hard question every morning has made me feel as if the project—and my part in it—has been purposeful. All I can say is keep the questions coming!"

MAKE IT A HABIT
ASSESS YOUR MOTIVATORS
STEPS FOR SUCCESS

After you have read through this chapter, answer the Personal Motivation Assessment Questions to identify the primary types of motivators that influence your emotions, thoughts, and behaviors.

Remember there are no right or wrong answers. Your purpose is to begin reshaping your own behavior by using a reinforcing motivator to reward yourself as you are successful.

EXERCISE 1:
IDENTIFY YOUR KEY MOTIVATORS

Once you've asked yourself the Personal Motivator Questions found in this chapter, record your results below. Mark all that apply, putting a star next to the motivational types you think describe you best.

- ☐ I am motivated by driving force.
- ☐ I am motivated by arousal.
- ☐ I am motivated by intrinsic factors.
- ☐ I am motivated by attention.
- ☐ I am motivated by avoidance.
- ☐ I am motivated by self-actualization.

EXERCISE 2:
IDENTIFY YOUR PARTNER'S KEY MOTIVATORS

Once you have identified your key motivators, sit with your partner and have them answer the Personal Motivator Questions and record their results below. Compare personal motivation assessments.

The insights gained from the comparison may reveal core issues of contention that, once identified, could lead to better understanding of each other. For instance, there would be a lack of satisfaction and palpable tension in a relationship where one person is motivated by a need for attention, and the other person is motivated by avoidance.

Discuss how you might work together, given each of your key motivational factors, to help each other grow in your relationship.

Mark all that apply, putting a star next to the motivational types you think describe you the best.

- ☐ I am motivated by driving force.
- ☐ I am motivated by arousal.
- ☐ I am motivated by intrinsic factors.
- ☐ I am motivated by attention.
- ☐ I am motivated by avoidance.
- ☐ I am motivated by self-actualization.

Chapter 8
CHOICES

Freedom in Options

DEFERRING

"I've worked in construction all my life." Eduardo shared. "I'm pretty good at hanging drywall. Plus, I'm fast and efficient, and my bosses have always appreciated my work ethic," Eduardo added with a measure of pride.

Eduardo told me about his job and why he came to see me that morning. He explained that his boss had hired a new guy named Dan to help him. Dan was supposed to be experienced working with drywall—at least he said he was. Dan had an associate's degree in construction management. Eduardo had never finished high school. Dan talked about how he was trained in how to plan, schedule, and control construction projects. Eduardo thought surely Dan must have also learned the importance of doing a job well with accuracy and good time management. But that was not the case.

Eduardo was uncomfortable. This new guy talked big about his skills. He challenged Eduardo the first time he met him—in front of the site foreman, no less.

As he surveyed the half-finished room, Dan said, "It took you all day to hang these walls? Man, I could have done this job in half that time!"

Being soft spoken, Eduardo looked down and said nothing. He looked up to see the foreman pause. He had a questioning look on his face.

"Really? Half the time?" the foreman said. "Okay, Eduardo. Why don't you let him take the lead today? Maybe you'll learn a few new tricks." The foreman directed the men to begin working and then walked away to another part of the job site.

Dan flashed an arrogant smile and said, "Come on Eduardo, let me teach you a few new tricks!"

It's going to be a long day, Eduardo thought to himself.

WHEN TO EAT, WHEN NOT TO EAT

"I can't figure out the best way to help my seven-year-old son, Tommy, make the right choice every time something comes up. And things come up all the time!" Tom exclaimed one day in session. "I mean, come on! One day, just out of the blue, my son declared, "No dinner!" He decided to make his own rule that he wouldn't eat dinner unless we're all sitting at the table together. What am I supposed to do with that?" Tom went on, "There are times I don't get home until eight or nine o'clock at night. Tommy, Jr.'s, bedtime is eight o'clock. When I don't get home until after he's asleep, how is that going to work? He needs to eat dinner before he goes to bed!"

Tom and his wife, Mary, were extremely frustrated with their son's behavior. Mary tried everything to get Tommy to eat dinner, but he wouldn't eat a bite. She coaxed him, fixed his favorite meals, and even punished him. But Tommy was determined. He was not going to sit at the table unless Daddy was at the dinner table, too. Tommy resorted to eating a larger-than-usual snack after school. In the evening, he would defiantly refuse to sit at the table for dinner until Tom came home. Tommy would entertain himself until it was his bedtime. Then he would go to his room and crawl into bed at eight o'clock. Tommy's hunger strike had gone on for three weeks. Tom and Mary had no idea what to do about the situation.

After hearing about Tom and Mary's frustrating parenting situation with Tommy, I wanted to offer them some help. I asked them if they had ever heard of the concept of providing "forced-choice options" for their son. Tom said he had never heard of the concept but was willing to try anything at this point.

THE POWER OF CHOICE

Our choices are made based on our personal perceptions, and perception is all a matter of perspective. Eduardo and the new guy on the job had differing personal perceptions, similar to Tom and his son. An individual's perspective is formed from a person's own evaluation of a situation or fact (from their own point of view). In Eduardo's case, the new guy thought he could do the job better than Eduardo. Eduardo had a different point of view. In Tom's case, Tommy made what he thought was his best choice not to eat so that he could get his father's attention to spend more time with him.

The choices we make are based on the personal perceptions we have formed by our own understanding and discerning of the information we have received.

The power of perception means we have the ability, skill, or capacity to become aware by understanding and discernment. When we have a particular point of view on a situation, however, that view may be limited. We may lack a measure of ability or skill in understanding, and this lack limits our awareness. It is important to expand our perspective to develop our own personal power of perception. This is particularly important when dealing with the motivations associated with our making choices.

The evaluation of any situation which requires us to make choices also requires us to look at all aspects of the circumstances, considering and examining them to establish their value in our lives.

In 1956, Benjamin S. Bloom identified a need to approach the three domains of learning—*cognitive, affective, and psychomotor*—through an organizational construct. He thoughtfully categorized the learning process as a hierarchy, thus identifying it as a sequence from understanding fully through to establishing personal value as applied to any idea or concept.

We can summarize the steps of this process as follows:

» Knowledge or General Awareness—

 The first step in the hierarchy of choice is to know the basics of the situation, concept, or idea. Knowledge gives us the general awareness of information, facts, or, ideas regarding the topic.

» Grasping Meaning/Comprehension—

 The second step is to comprehend or understand each person's role in the situation. When comprehension occurs, it means we have grasped the meaning of what has occurred or is occurring.

» Application and Finding Relevance—

 The next step is to look at the particular situation at hand and assign its relevance to ourselves or to the specific area or circumstance. This step is called "application."

» Analysis of Parts—

 Once the particulars of the situation are understood, it is important to analyze or look at all the issues being presented. Analysis means we can separate out portions of a concept or a situation to examine all its parts independently.

» Synthesis—

 Next, it is important to synthesize the situation. The process of synthesis means we are able to combine or delete different ideas, concepts, or parts to create a new whole.

» Evaluation/Considering Value—

It is at this point in the full process where an informed evaluation to establish value can be made regarding any situation or choice.[1]

EMPOWERED TO CHOOSE

We already mentioned that power is the developed ability, skill, and capacity to make positive choices. Therefore, to feel "empowered to choose," means to make choices from a sense of confidence or positive self-esteem concerning those developments.

Sometimes a lack of performance is perceived as a lack of ability, but this perception is not accurate. Sometimes the person expected to perform does not fully see or understand the value of succeeding in developing additional options. It can be easier to fall back on enacting choices that may be limiting, yet are familiar, rather than to come up with other possible options.

FREEDOM IN OPTIONS

There is great importance in expanding perspective to develop personal power of perception, specifically in the area of developing options for choice making. In this section, the topic of options is discussed in relation to the concept of experiential blindness.

The term, "experiential blindness" was first coined by MIT Philosophy Professor Alva Noe regarding a phenomenon as evidence for a relationship between sensorimotor skills and perceptual experience. The hypothesis of *experiential blindness* is that there is the interdependence of perception and action.

Noe explains, "Perception is not a process in the brain, but a kind of skillful activity of the body as a whole. We enact our perceptual experience." In other words, if one does not perceive something, that is, if the idea or concept is not in their conscious awareness, they do not have the ability to act based on that which they do not know.[2]

With experiential blindness in mind, the goal is to expand our perspective and become experientially aware. As we increase the size, extent, or scope of our awareness, a wider variety of options present themselves along with our expanded perspective. As we gain more options and the freedom of choice, we are able to fully determine our preferences in any given situation and choose that which is more desirable to us personally.

Therefore, the idea of developing options based on experiential awareness, allows someone to act on that which is more desirable without restraint or restriction. However, not everyone understands that there is a wide range of options available to them. Also, not everyone believes they are empowered to exercise the right to choose. And too, even if certain individuals believed they were able to choose freely, some, who do not feel a sense of personal empowerment or who suffer from low self-esteem, believe that their desires do not hold value.

Further, desire without restraint or restriction can sometimes be perceived as lacking structure. People function better when there is structure to their choice making. We see this structure play out in the grocery store or restaurants one frequents. We get in the habit of repeating the choices we make. Breaking out of the habit of this type of choice making can be quite distressing for someone who believes there are limits to their options.

A mindset shift is to consider the possibility that multiple options for choice making are available at all times. Old emotions, behaviors, and motives related to past choices do not have to be repeated. Consider that everyone can become empowered and exercise the right to choose alternative options in any circumstance.

As one finds success with their choices, they are able to attain a measure of confidence or self-esteem regarding the continued use of options. The successful outcomes of varied options increase experiences, expands options further, and, in turn, expands a person's behavioral actions. Desire without restraint or restriction related to experiencing new choice options can exist within a safe frame and structure.

This consideration of possibilities promotes awareness. Through this awareness alone, one takes a step closer to acquiring power and developing the ability, skill, and capacity to develop choice options effectively.

BEST CHOICES

Determining "best choices" is more complicated. We all like to make the right choice the first time around in any given situation. Taking the time to investigate and explore the possibilities of new options is important. The process for determining the "best choices" is to seek the most outstanding options that hold the highest degree of excellence for a given situation.

So where does one go to overcome experiential blindness in contexts of developing new options for choice making? A good place to start an investigation on where these new options can be experienced is within a person's own sphere of influence.

Look around at others with whom you share a connection. Look to fellow tradesmen in construction. How do they onboard a new worker? Look to the family you admire. How do they parent a strong-willed child? The act of seeking alternatives promotes awareness on how others might handle choice making in a given situation.

This new search may prove that there are few individuals within the personal sphere of influence that consistently choose the best option in any given situation. However, there may be one or two people within this circle worthy of observing. Are these individuals empowered to make wise and positive choices within a safe structure consistently? Do they exercise their right and choose an alternative, yet positive means of choice making? Are they confident in their choice making? These are the people to learn from when trying to figure out the best option for making choices in a given situation.

Also, look to individuals and options outside the personal sphere of influence. There are educational courses, mentors, therapists, and programs within each community that serve to expand personal experiences leading to new options to consider. Most times the options offered through these avenues are thoughtfully organized and follow a sequence of skill development.

Understand your own sense of "best." By expanding your perspective through allowing new experiences into your life, developing personal power, and knowing that there is freedom in options, most anyone can make a quality choice.

CHOOSING TO MENTOR

The next day, after the group session, Eduardo went to work. Within a few minutes of arriving on the job site, he could tell by how Dan handled the tools and the drywall that he was all talk. This guy couldn't teach Eduardo anything new. In fact, if given a chance, Eduardo could teach Dan a few new tricks.

For most of the morning, Eduardo chose to say nothing. After assessing the lack of ability, he began to look at the situation through Dan's perspective. He was new. He was trying to make an impression, and he had probably had some difficulty finding work in the past. Eduardo began thinking about the best way to be gentle and caring in this situation rather than being arrogant and forceful with Dan.

At mid-morning break, Eduardo went to the food truck and bought snacks and iced tea for himself and for Dan. He pulled up a seat next to Dan in the room where they were working. Between bites and sips, Eduardo commented. "The foreman comes by while we're off at lunch and inspects the work every day." Eduardo took another sip of the tea and chose to dive into the conversation and perhaps do a little mentoring. "You know, if you look at the drywall that was hung here from yesterday, and you look at what we just did, they look different, don't you think?"

Eduardo let the comment hang between them as he finished his snack. He walked over to the last panel of drywall that he put up. "It is going to be important that we go back to each panel and check for screws." Eduardo took a putty knife and dragged it over each screw head and listened for clicks of metal contacting with metal. No sound was heard. "Ahhh. That's nice. Do you hear that? Nothing! No screw heads sticking out," he laughed.

Then he walked over to the last panel of drywall the new guy put up. Again, he dragged the putty knife over each screw head and listened.

Ting, scrape, ting, scrape, ting, scrape, over every single screw on the panel. All the screw heads were protruding past the surface of the drywall.

Immediately Dan started making excuses. The drywall was not the right size. The screws were too long—on and on Dan went.

Eduardo patiently listened and went on coaching. "See how this joint compound here is too thick?" Eduardo pointed to a section of the drywall-taping the new guy just finished. "We need to redo this section," he said calmly. "We don't want the foreman seeing this while we're gone. He's just going to make us redo it anyway!"

Eduardo got up and began to work on Dan's mistakes. With the electric screwdriver, Eduardo quickly, expertly drove the screws deeper into place on the last panel. He took a scraper and removed the uneven joint compound from around the panel, and scooped some joint compound out of the pail and put it into a smaller bucket. He thinned out the gooey mixture with a bit of water, stirring it to the desired consistency. "See all of these bumps and blobs?" he said to Dan. "Before you start taping, you have to thin and mix the joint compound. If you take it straight from the bucket, it doesn't spread evenly."

Without looking back, Eduardo held up the knife in the air to show Dan how to handle the tool. He applied the thinner compound smoothly and added, "Remember to run your taping knife over all the joints when the compound dries. You want to knock off all the ridges, even the ones you can't see."

As Eduardo finished the coaching moment, he turned to find the foreman standing behind Dan. He wasn't sure how long he had been standing there, but the foreman was smiling broadly.

"This job needs to be finished today, guys. Doesn't look like you two are going to make it if Eduardo has to do his work and yours!" The foreman looked sternly at Dan who was still seated on the crate with a mouth full of potato chips.

"He's got this. We've got this, boss." Eduardo shot back as he nudged Dan to his feet.

"You'd better, or heads will roll," the foreman said with a twinkle in his eye. "Eduardo, take the lead and show this rookie a thing or two, would ya? I'll be back for inspection at noon." The foreman turned to leave with a chuckle.

Dan turned to Eduardo. "Hey, thanks man." There was a measure of humility in his voice that wasn't there before.

"No problem." Eduardo was proud of himself for making a choice to be kind, caring, and mentoring. He remembered how hard it was to be the new guy looking for a break. "Now let's get back to work."

TAKE YOUR PICK

During our session, I explained to Tom that a forced-choice option refers to a specific and direct way to help parents achieve a desired behavioral response from their children. The parent provides two or three options for the child. The child then must select one of the options presented.

Offering a limited number of parent-driven choices encourages a child to consider their possibilities and take action, while the child experiences a measure of cooperative control in the process.

As we concluded our session, I asked Tom, "What time can you and Mary both be available to spend time with your son on a daily basis?"

Tom thought for a moment. There was the time in the morning before he left for work and Tommy went to school. Mary got breakfast together for the family then. Maybe he and Tommy could have fun in the kitchen together in the morning.

There was also lunch time. Mary was available every day during lunch. Tom couldn't get away from work every day, but he could take off at least one day a week to meet Tommy and Mary at school for lunchtime.

Tom agreed to talk to his wife about the forced-choice options idea. Tom still wasn't sure how it would all work, but he was encouraged when he left my office that day.

Tom came to the next session happy and content. He said that Tommy's hunger strike was over. The forced-choice option worked.

Tom shared that he and Mary decided to sit Tommy down and emphasize the importance of eating his evening meal. They explained that having dinner together at night didn't work for every member of the family, but they gave their son a choice about what he considered to be a better time for everyone to sit for a meal together. They gave him two options: Tom and Tommy could prepare breakfast together for the family every Monday through Thursday, or Tom and Mary would meet Tommy at his school on Wednesdays for lunch.

Tommy thought about his options. It didn't take him long to choose to prepare the breakfast meal Monday through Thursday. He rationalized his decision, saying that when he was at school, he liked to eat lunch with his friends, but in the morning, he could have his mom and dad all to himself.

Breakfast it was!

Mary started to use the forced-choice options with Tommy in other areas, too. Did he want to do his homework before dinner or after dinner? Did he want to take a morning shower or an evening shower? Did he prefer to do his chores on Monday, Wednesday, and Friday or Tuesday, Thursday, and Saturday?

Mary even started to use the forced-choice options with Tom, as well. Did he want to have date night on Friday or Saturday? Did he want to take care of cleaning out the garage Saturday or Sunday? Did he want to mow the lawn at the beginning of the week or in the middle to have more time on the weekends?

As Tom was leaving my office, he turned and said, "Thanks for all your help! Our mornings are a blast. Tommy and I are getting creative in the kitchen. Forced-choice options really work!" Tom chuckled, "And they work with me, too!"

MAKE IT A HABIT
CHOICES: FREEDOM IN OPTIONS
STEPS FOR SUCCESS

Take a look and examine your current choice-making decisions. Then consider expanding your options. Your basic purpose is to develop an extensive battery of options for any given situation. Remember to celebrate yourself as you are successful.

The exercises below walk you through an organizational construct; a sequence from understanding fully through to establishing personal value as applied to expanding choice-making options.

Once you're confident with your practice, you may want to inform your partner or friends about what you're doing and why you're doing it, so they can begin to help support you in your efforts.

EXERCISE 1 EXAMPLE: IDENTIFICATION

In the blank exercises that follow, pick an area of life where you would like to expand your choice-making options and write them down.

For example: house cleaning.

- » Make a list of current options available to you:
    - › Clean the whole house one day a week.
    - › Clean one room each day, taking no more than an hour to clean.
    - › Clean only certain rooms each week.
- » Come up with three additional options that you wouldn't normally consider.

- Hire a cleaning service once a month to do the deep cleaning.
- Have your spouse or partner help.
- Have your children help.

EXERCISE 2 EXAMPLE: DISCUSSION

Have a discussion with your spouse or partner and your children to consider the options. Make sure, when discussing the new options, everyone understands fully and sees the value of the new options posed. Help them by explaining the possibilities through the organizational construct:

- Knowledge or General Awareness—

  Lay out the basics of the situation.
  - The house requires upkeep and cleaning.
  - We all use each room of the house every day.
  - We all can share in the duty of cleaning.

- Grasping Meaning/Comprehension—

  Help each member of the family to understand each person's role in the family and in maintaining the goal.
  - Mom and dad work five days a week.
    - ☐ Work clothes require cleaning.
    - ☐ Rooms used throughout the week require cleaning.
  - Children attend school and after school activities.
    - ☐ School clothes and sports clothes require cleaning.

- ☐ Rooms used throughout the week require cleaning.

» Application and Finding Relevance—

The next step is to apply the new option.

> Mom will take care of the laundry for herself and the baby.

> Dad will take care of his own laundry.

> The two older children will learn to do their own laundry based on a list of duties to accomplish.

> Mom and Dad will share cleaning the master bedroom, bathroom, and baby's room.

> The two older children will clean their own rooms based on a list of duties to accomplish given by Mom and Dad.

> Two older children will share cleaning the guest bathroom and living room based on a list of duties to accomplish given by Mom and Dad.

EXERCISE 3 EXAMPLE: ANALYSIS, SYNTHESIS, AND EVALUATION

Have a weekly family meeting. Use the time to have each member of the family review their accomplishments with the new option put in place to clean the house. Log any changes that family members recommend to improve the process.

» Analysis of Parts—

Once every member of the family understands what is expected, it is important to look at the successes each week.

» Synthesis—

Talk through any changes that are required to tighten up the process.

» Evaluation/Considering Value—

Talk about the importance and value regarding the choice.

Celebrate the value and success of the house cleaning option. Keep the practice of meeting as a family going to support each other and to establish the practice as a habit for everyone.

EXERCISE 1:
IDENTIFICATION

Pick an area of life where you would like to expand your choice-making options: _____

Make a list of current options available to you.

» _____

_____

_____

» _____

_____

_____

» _____

_____

_____

Write three additional options you wouldn't normally consider.

» _____

_____

_____

» _____
  _____
  _____

» _____
  _____
  _____

EXERCISE 2: DISCUSSION

Have a discussion with your spouse or partner and your children to consider options. Make sure everyone understands fully and sees the value of the new options posed. Help by explaining the options through the organizational construct:

» Knowledge or General Awareness—

  Lay out the basics of the situation.

  › _____
    _____
    _____

  › _____
    _____
    _____

  › _____
    _____
    _____

» Grasping Meaning/Comprehension—

Help each member of the family to understand each person's role in the family and their specific role in maintaining the goal.

› _____

› _____

› _____

» Application and Finding Relevance—

The next step is to apply the new option.

› _____

› _____

› _____

EXERCISE 3:
ANALYSIS, SYNTHESIS, AND EVALUATION

Have a weekly family meeting. Use the time to have each member of the family review their accomplishments with the new option put in place to complete the task at hand. Log any changes that family members recommend to improve the process.

» Analysis of Parts—

Once every member of the family understands what is expected, it is important to look at the successes each week.

» Synthesis—

Talk through any changes that are required to tighten up the process.

» Evaluation/Considering Value—

Talk about the importance and value regarding the choice.

Celebrate the value and success of the option. Keep the practice of meeting as a family going to support each other and securely set the practice into a habit for everyone.

Chapter 9
HABITS

Break Old Ones;
Create New Ones

STRESS-INDUCED SELF-ABSORPTION

Jason sat uncomfortably erect in his chair during the group session. "I have such a bad habit," Jason exclaimed. "I talk on and on to my wife. She sits there patiently *for a while*. Then she explodes." Jason's sat stiffly with his hands in his lap and his fingers tightly interlocked. His attempts to demonstrate assurance and control fell short, as his knee bounced out a rhythm to an unheard double-bass beat.

"How long is *'a while,'* Jason?" I asked.

"Well, I can go on. Sometimes I talk for a couple hours."

"Hmmm," I said, "And during that time does your wife ever have the opportunity to talk?"

Jason looked down at his hands, white knuckles protruding from pressure. Then he let go of his grip and pushed down on both legs attempting to quiet his bouncing knee. "No. She sits there watching me. She nods sometimes and says, *'Hmm,' 'yes,'* or *'I see.'* She's so patient—until she isn't anymore."

Jason went on to explain that after a while she just screams, *"ENOUGH!"* and leaves to go lie down in the other room.

"Are you ever curious about what she thinks during your conversations? Does she ever have a chance to share her point of view with you?"

Jason looked up at me. "You know, this may sound selfish, but I don't care to hear what she has to say. I am so stressed with what I am dealing with that I just need her to listen. I guess it's just my habit to come home and unload on her." Tears started to run down his cheeks.

THE HABIT OF BEING RIGHT

Reese was determined to press her point. "It's not fair," she told me.

And Reese was always right when it came to fairness. She knew it, so everyone should know it, too. In our time together, Reese confided in me that she wouldn't stop pressing an issue in a conversation until the other person conceded. Even if they left the conversation unconvinced, she was still sure she was right. When something wasn't fair, she wouldn't let go of the issue until fairness, according to her standards, was restored.

Reese related to me that she first noticed this tendency about a year ago when she decided to go to night school to get her associate's degree in nursing. At the beginning of her second year, though, she was discouraged by the responses she had gotten from her professors. They had all given her low marks on her papers and for class participation.

"I just don't understand," Reese said with an incredulous tone. "I write very well and participate all the time in every class!" Running her fingers through her hair and rolling her eyes, she continued her story. "There are people in the class who say nothing. I don't get why they're getting better grades than me."

I looked up from my notes, "Have you spoken to your professors one on one, to get a better sense of why you're getting the grades you're getting?"

"Of course," Reese stated, as though I should already have known this about her situation. "At the end of last year, I went to each of the professors' offices nearly every week."

"What was their feedback?"

Again, running her fingers through her hair and rolling her eyes, she said, "I was told by all four professors that I needed to spend more time listening and less time confronting them and what they were teaching. But really, if they're teaching wrong, shouldn't someone tell them?"

"What do you mean by 'teaching wrong'?"

"Well, for instance… if I have to give patients bad news about their conditions, I am not going to coddle them. I'm going to come right out and tell them. One professor wants us to sit by a patient's bedside, meet them eye to eye, maybe even take their hand, and then deliver the bad news." Reese looked a bit uncomfortable with my line of questioning. "Being direct is the right thing to do. Right?"

WHAT MAKES A HABIT A HABIT?

Both Jason and Reese developed habits that did not serve them well. The good news was that they had the ability to change up their negative habits and replace them with new and improved ones. A habit is an automatic tendency or practice based on context clues. It's a thought or behavior that is regular, settled, known, and repeated over and over again. Habits don't just develop overnight. They evolve from past thoughts or behaviors over time, and, once established, habits are hard to give up. Habitual thoughts and behaviors follow a pattern and are repeated time and time again with a set sequence or a regular routine. Although developed over a continued period of time, there is an impulsive, unconscious quality to habits that make them require little effort or thinking. Our habits seem to be instinctual.

In 2006, a group of researchers that crossed "the Pond," between London and California, collaborated to study the influence of context clues and goals on habitual performance. The research of noted psychologists Neal, Wood, Wu, and Kurlander, from 2006 through 2012, pointed to the idea that habits are activated directly by context cues, with minimal influence of goals.[1] As a result, Neal, et. al. attempted to clarify how habits become habits, with a secondary focus of separating out and measuring the independent influences of context clues vs. goals on habit performance. In the end, these studies supported previously conducted theoretical and conceptual analysis which found that our habits represent a goal-independent form of automaticity.[2]

Furthering these findings, two additional studies were conducted by the trio of Gardner, Lally, and Wardle. Their work supported the theory, in regard to behavioral change, that, as automaticity of behavior increases—that is, *the more automatic it becomes*—enactment of the behavior becomes more comfortable. They found that behavior directed by habit is regulated by impulse and is detached from motivational or volitional control.[3]

As these researchers continued their work through the studies of habit formation in general practice. Additional research sought to break down the way habits are formed and recreate the process to bring about desired changes in behavior through the formation of new habits. The outcome of their work led to the suggestion that professionals could consider providing habit-formation strategies and guidance as a way to promote long-term behavior change. The recommended strategy to bring about such change proposed three phases: *an initiation phase, a learning phase, and a stability phase.*[4]

PUTTING THE HABIT-FORMATION STRATEGY TO WORK FOR YOU

Specifically for our purposes, this three-phase habit-formation strategy can be applied to communication development and growth.

Here's an example of the process of forming a new communication habit:

» The Problem:

I have a tendency to be sharp and curt (brisk, cutting, abrupt, appearing rude) with my tone and communication when leading my team of employees. I am not trying to be rude. My intention with this behavior is based on the belief that time is money. I am wanting to save myself and others time, so they, and I, can get back to focus on the task at hand. Long-time employees are starting to quit. New employees are afraid of me. I am creating an uncomfortable, hostile work environment, when what I really seek to create is a productive workplace. As the leader, I want to focus on improving my communication by expressing information in a quality manner.

» In the Initiation Phase, where habit formation around a communication strategy begins:

> First, a desired new communication strategy is selected.

☐ *I have decided to focus on changing my sharp and curt tone.*

> Next, the context in which the communication strategy will be enacted is selected.

☐ *The context where my new communication pattern will be enacted is in the workplace with my employees.*

» In the Learning Phase, where the habit-formation process develops:

> The communication strategy is repeated in the chosen context.

☐ *For one week, I will focus on and write down how many times a day I find myself communicating with a sharp or curt tone with my employees.*

> Then the habit process of the new communication strategy is strengthened by the context-behavior association.

For four weeks, I will focus on communicating by putting the following in place:

- ☐ *Offering clear and compound sentences, instead of using one-word commands or answers.*
- ☐ *Making eye contact when someone speaks to me, instead of continuing what I am doing.*
- ☐ *Asking questions to assess my accuracy and receptivity of the employee's communication with me.*
- ☐ *Each day I will write down the changes I see in myself and others with the intent to identify the strengths of my new habit and to assess the level of how naturally it now occurs (the automaticity) that has developed in my new communication strategy.*

» Finally, in the Stability Phase, consistently using the communication strategy:

› This is where the habit forms, and its strength plateaus over time with minimal effort or deliberation.

- ☐ *I will look back at my writing and note specific examples and patterns related to my using the new communication strategy.*

GIVING TO RECEIVE

After only a few different group sessions, Jason became more aware that his selfishness was causing the problem between him and his wife. He had been relying on her good nature and patience to satisfy his own need to vent. He was ready to change his habit of verbally dumping on his wife each and every night.

Jason set his intention to focus on coming into the house differently after work. He wanted to change his tendency to walk in the door, drop his briefcase and coat, and yell, "Honey, are you home?" He knew she was always going to answer with, "Yes, I'm here," and come meet him at the door.

With the group's guidance, Jason came up with three positive communication behaviors he wanted to commit to habit. He came to realize that, although he called his wife "Honey," it wasn't very respectful to pair the term of endearment with a yell as soon as he got home. He finally understood that his shouting could be miscommunicated as, *'Now that I'm here, you need to drop whatever you're doing, and give me all your attention.'*

He came to see that it would be more respectful to enter the house quietly, go to his wife, and pair the word, "Honey," with a second word, phrase, or action of endearment. Jason decided the second part should be something physical. He determined that when he got home each day, he would go to his wife, wherever she was in the house, walk up to her and extend his arms with the intention to embrace her. He would then say, *"Hi Honey, how was your day?"* The third part of his habit change was going to be listening to what she had to say first, before he started talking.

A few weeks later Jason looked lighter, less stressed. He began to share. Before he started to change his habits around communication, he thought the suggestions we came up with were a bit cheesy. But his wife didn't feel that way when he began to put them into practice.

Jason sat still and calm as he related what happened to the group. "The first time I walked into the house and found my wife at the kitchen sink. She panicked at seeing me. She asked if something was wrong." Jason's eyes filled. "All I did was hold out my arms, and she fell into me. Then I said the rehearsed line, 'Hi Honey, how was your day?' She pulled back from the hug and looked at me with surprise."

Jason went on to tell how his wife found it odd that he should be asking about her because he never did. He let her in on the way he was working on the new habit he was attempting to develop. Jason said his wife smiled from ear to ear! She couldn't wait until they started to practice together.

As time passed, Jason found it became easier and easier to focus on what his wife was sharing. He was less inclined to stay stressed about his day. There were even nights when he didn't share about his day at all, because his wife's day was so interesting. His wife was happy, and their marriage began to thrive.

LETTING GO OF ALWAYS BEING RIGHT

It took a bit of conversation to help Reese consider the possibility that the communication difficulty had more to do with her than her professors. With a fair amount of introspection, Reese acknowledged that she experienced similar conflict with most people around communication. Her need to be right often stopped her from being flexible and open to other perspectives and points of view.

Reese became more aware that her belief that she was right was naturally categorizing *everyone else as wrong*. Professors stopped attempting to teach her new material given her fixed mindset. Reese was smart enough to realize they had stopped teaching, but what was finally becoming clear to her was why they had stopped working with her. Reese wanted to be a nurse; however, our sessions had helped her discover that she had to change her habits of having to be right all the time. She had to let her professors know she was teachable.

Reese began this process by setting her intentions to collect information from multiple sources *before* formulating an opinion about an issue. She thought it best to record who she was citing to support her point of view. She worked hard to refrain from talking in class unless her point of view was not expressed in the discussion by other students.

After setting this new habit-development strategy into motion, Reese approached her first semester differently that year. She walked into class, sat in her chair, and wrote down what the professor and her fellow students discussed. In the evenings she would research what was discussed and add more notes to what she had already written. Learning became exciting to Reese. After a few classes had passed Reese noticed her professors were treating her differently. They were asking her what she thought on the subjects presented. Her papers were being returned with the grades she thought she should earn based upon her efforts.

At the end of the semester, Reese entered our group session in such a positive mood. Her entire appearance had changed. She was quiet and relaxed. There was no hair tossing or eye rolling. Reese had earned straight A's for the term, and she was extremely proud of herself.

Reese went on to explain that she had to eat humble pie and change her way of thinking. She finally realized that she wasn't always *right,* because her being right made everyone else *wrong*—even the professors who really did know more than she did.

As Reese focused on maintaining a learning mindset, wrote down everything shared in class, and conducted research at night, her knowledge base changed. She was indeed learning new and different ways of thinking, being, and communicating. She developed a great rapport with her professors and found that as she opened herself to listening, the professors were more inclined to teach her.

MAKE IT A HABIT
BREAK OLD HABITS; MAKE NEW ONES
STEPS FOR SUCCESS

After you have set your intention to develop new habit patterns and strengthen your communication skills, use the following exercises to guide you.

You may want to inform your partner or friends about what you're doing and why you're doing it so they can begin to help support you in your efforts.

Remember the three-phase habit-formation strategy as you seek to break old negative communication patterns and develop new positive ones.

EXERCISE 1: COMMUNICATION QUIZ

To develop new communication skills in your life, start by assessing where your strengths and weaknesses lie. The following is a list of questions to ask yourself about your communication level. Take personal inventory on which areas you have a handle on and can respond with a resounding 'yes'. Consider if each item is working for you or not.

Answer the following questions with a simple "yes" or "no."

RECEPTION/EXPRESSION

Yes   No   I am able to actively listen.

Yes   No   I receive information accurately.

Yes   No   I express information in a quality manner.

EMOTION

Yes   No   I am comfortable with and understand all of my emotions when communicating.

Yes   No   I have self-control over my emotions when communicating.

Yes   No   I am able to express and communicate my emotions clearly.

BEHAVIOR

Yes   No   I know that behaviors can exist alone when communicating.

Yes   No   I can make the distinction between behavior and emotion when communicating.

Yes   No   I am able to positively change my behavior using restraint and recovery when communicating.

MOTIVATION

Yes No I understand the concept of motivation related to communication.

Yes No I am aware of what motivates me to communicate.

Yes No I am able to alter my motivation when communicating.

CHOICES

Yes No I have the ability, skill, and capacity to make choices in communication.

Yes No I am able to make positive choice options when communicating.

Yes No I am able to discern the "best choices" regarding personal communication.

How did you do? For which areas can you say, "Yes, I have this down?" In which areas do you need to focus and strengthen your skills?

EXERCISE 2: FORM A NEW HABIT

After taking the Communication Quiz, set your intention to focus working on one identified communication area or idea. Develop your new habit-formation communication strategy around that area or idea, using the template below.

INITIATION PHASE

» I will focus on:_____

_____

_____

» The context in which the new communication strategy will be enacted is: _____

_____

_____

LEARNING PHASE

» For one week I will focus on and write down: _____

_____

_____

» For four weeks I will focus on communicating by putting the following in place: _____

_____

_____

» Each day I will write down the changes I see in myself and others with the intent to identify the strength and level of the automatic habit process of the new strategy.

STABILITY PHASE

» I will look back at my writing and note examples and patterns related to using the new communication strategy.

Challenge yourself to develop new communication habits. Once you hit your stride, attempt to integrate one positive communication strategy into your habits each month. Practice new habit-formation strategies for three months, six months, or a year. Observe your success with changing communication for the better. You may wish to see what becomes of the targeted changes after a year in review. See how the people around you respond to your newly developed style of communication. Have fun with the process.

Chapter 10
FOCUS ON SMALL SUCCESSES

Take Care of Your Next Minute

HOPELESS AFTER THREE YEARS

David knew he had to change how he treated his wife of three years. Colleen had had just about enough. She was spending less and less time at the house when he was there. David knew she was ready to pack her belongings and leave.

David didn't want Colleen to go. Since their wedding day, he had denied, minimized, or rationalized his negative behavior toward her. He and Colleen got along so well prior to getting married. They dated for four years. During that time, they shared wonderful times together. They were both kind and supportive of one another. David wasn't clear on why things had changed so dramatically once they got married.

He related to me that he had started to act like his father, something he did not want to do. He perceived his father as unkind and cruel. His father was an entitled man who thought he had power and privilege over his mother. And his mother went right along with it, as well. His father would bark an order, and his mother would immediately respond by doing whatever he was barking about. There was a generational and cultural support that legitimized or excused his father's pattern of treating his mother like a maid, housekeeper, and childcare provider.

Over the last three years, David increasingly saw his father in himself. Something had to change. *He* had to change. His marriage depended upon it.

David sat in session with a minimum of emotional expression. He spoke in a monotone voice with diminished facial expressions. He appeared apathetic. I could tell that hopelessness was setting in. He perked up a bit with my mention of putting a behavioral strategy in place. He was willing to do what he could to save his marriage and win Colleen's heart back once again.

DESTRUCTIVE PATTERNS OF ABUSE

Paulette and Howard had struggled over their nine years of marriage. Both came from dysfunctional and violent homes. As a child, Paulette was neglected. She had gone most days without an evening meal, roaming the streets by day, putting herself to bed, starting at an early age, while her parents drank themselves into a rage before falling off to sleep. Howard experienced similar struggles as a child. Along with the neglect, Howard suffered weekly beatings from his out-of-control, alcoholic father.

Here they sat together in a session. They had five children under the age of eight. The children were at home supervised by the assigned respite-care social worker. Paulette and Howard acknowledged they were repeating the nightmare chaos they both experienced as children. They drank, fought, and were violent with each other. They were also filled with remorse and shame because they behaved this way in front of their children. Neither could remember what they made for dinner the night before for the little ones. Their situation had come to the point that Social Services was intervening in their family's lives for a fourth time over the years.

Paulette and Howard professed their love for each other and their children. And they both knew that their childhood experiences could not be used to explain, excuse, or condone their current behavior and the present violence in their home. A change was necessary for them to retain parental rights of their children. The destructive impact of their behavior and the use of violence had created negative effects on Paulette's and Howard's self-esteem, on their affection toward each other and their children, and upon the perceptions of their children who were third-generation witnesses and victims of the domestic-violence cycle. The couple knew that the impact of the situation was in direct conflict with responsible parenting, but they felt powerless to change.

The couple had two weeks before they were to meet with a mediator. Social Services would be in attendance. If a positive change was not evidenced, Social Services intended to start the process to remove their parental rights. Paulette and Howard were motivated to put a behavioral strategy into place. They were primed and ready to take care of their next minute and focus on small successes over the next two weeks. They wanted to show the mediator, the social worker, the judge, and most importantly, themselves, that they could learn how to be responsible parents.

THE POWER OF REINFORCEMENT

How have you been successful today? This week? The question of your next-minute success is fundamental. Neither David or Paulette and Howard could answer these questions. If you focus on developing the habit of the successful use of positive strategies each week—for a minute, a week, a month, three months, six months, a year—*classic, operant, and observational conditioning* suggests that, thereafter, your focus will remain on the habits these positive strategies have created.

There are three main elements, or conditions, to this behavioral theory.[1,2]

1. ***Classical conditioning*** refers to a traditional state of existence. Basically, this means when you put two behaviors together at the same time, a response occurs. One of the behaviors is neutral or uncharged. The other behavior is

stimulating in some way, which rouses or spurs something to occur within you.

2. **Operant conditioning** means *the existence of a consequence following a behavior*. This infers that behavior is a result of external forces. These forces can be reinforcing or punitive. Reinforcing circumstances strengthen behaviors, while punitive consequences cause us to withdraw from the behaviors that brought them about. In other words, some behaviors have positive consequences that cause us to want to repeat them. Conversely, some behaviors net us negative consequences, causing us to want to avoid those behaviors in the future.

3. **Observational conditioning** means *learning from watching*. This idea supports that people are greatly influenced by their environment. Environmental exposure leads people to imitate, mimic, or copy the same behaviors they have seen in the past.

For this chapter, our focus will be on *operant conditioning*. *Operant conditioning* is a learning process in which new behaviors are acquired and modified through their association with consequences. As stated above, consequences can either serve to reinforce or punish us. The goal is to reinforce the desired behavior. This goal increases the likelihood the desired behavior will occur again in the future. If neutral or negative reinforcers are used, they serve to punish the behavior. This negativity decreases the likelihood that you will attend to actively changing unwanted behaviors in the future.

Scheduled reinforcement (planning when and how reinforcers will occur) is an essential component of the learning process. When and how often we reinforce a behavior can have a dramatic impact on the strength and rate of the desired positive response.

POSITIVE REINFORCEMENT

It is important to note that *positive reinforcement* is not to be confused with *false reinforcement*. *Positive reinforcement* focuses attention (the reinforcer) on the desired or preferred outcome. *False reinforcement* is feedback that is not in accord with what is really truth or fact. This false feedback gives an inflated perception of the value, contributions, level of performance, or success of the targeted behavior.

The potential impact of *false reinforcement* includes:

» *Confusion* in perception, communication, and, ultimately, the understanding of and acquiring of success. An individual will not improve their performance or achieve success when they have a misguided belief that they are already being successful.

» *Lack of trust and confidence* in the process or person providing the reinforcement. Most people are aware of their shortcomings. When they are positively reinforced for what they know to be a failure, skepticism sets in.

» *Reduction in the motivation* of someone who would benefit from constructive feedback to grow personally.

» *Conflicting messaging* makes it difficult in the communication process to hold one's self and others accountable.

Conversely, *positive reinforcement* serves to:

» *Offer clarity,* giving the person the opportunity to focus directly on improving performance toward success.

» *Build trust and confidence* in the change process, and one learns to recognize and focus on their self-generated success.

» *Motivate* the individual to seek out and benefit from constructive feedback to grow personally.

» *Provide clear messaging* to hold an individual accountable.

It is important to provide positive reinforcement comments every time, for 'effort' and 'growth from the baseline' rather than only for expected, predetermined, externally imposed outcomes. Small success is still a success. When external expectancies are imposed, the learner never has to problem solve, think through steps, or come up with personal solutions. The learner looks outward instead of inward for reward, seeking only to hit the predetermined goal. Always looking for external reward leads to learned helplessness. Learned helplessness is a frame of mind where a person suffers from and struggles with a sense of powerlessness. Often, this learned behavior is from a traumatic event, or, in this instance, a persistent failure to access success.

The goal is to empower yourself—to learn to fish rather than having been given a fish for one meal. The goal is to explore your own personal core issues so that you wrestle with your current abilities. Then you can find the entirety of them, determine a self-generated solution, and eventually realize your own successes.

We know that slips, regressions, errors, less than stellar accomplishments, not attending to the intended goal… are all indicators of something else. They stem from resistance, pain, fear, or a lack of confidence. It is important to acknowledge and accept yourself right where you are and then reinforce the steps of the task to be done. Only then can you begin the struggle of the thing you are wanting to change. With this strategy, you become your own change agent, while developing strategies to self-support and reinforce the fact that *you can do it!*

There is always something to find in a conversation, an event, a text, in your writing, that is inherently good and can be positively reinforced. Everyone—without exception—wants to be valued, understood, and appreciated. It is best to start with valuing, understanding, and appreciating yourself—even in the smallest of victories.

PUTTING FOCUS TO WORK FOR YOU

To start, focus on your next minute. Yes, your next minute.

A large part of developing a new personal, comfortable, positive strategy will be determined by the measure of success one gains from that strategy. If in the beginning, you put your full attention on taking care of each minute, by the time an hour passes you will realize that you have been successful for one full hour. This success in a short one hour is intrinsically rewarding. The reward serves as a spark to motivate you to continue the practice while increasing your time with success to two hours, a half of a day, the whole day.

You are intentionally, successfully, changing a habit using a behavioral strategy. We do it all the time!

Pick the best time of day to have a quiet fifteen minutes for this task. Think about what you want to focus on to positively reinforce. What thoughts, words, and or actions do you currently have that you want to change. Take no more than fifteen minutes. The time you pick might be in the morning, after your morning meal, at lunchtime, or sometime like the late afternoon, after dinner, or right before bedtime. Pick the best time for yourself to have a quiet fifteen minutes of time.

During this time think about that one thing you would like to change. It might be how you do, or do not, actively listen or express yourself in a conversation. It could be dealing with anxiety, frustration, or fear. It could be how you act with your intimate partner. Only you know what you need to change. Make sure your focus is on just one area that you desire to change. Then write your thoughts down, and each day for one week, take fifteen minutes to focus your attention on what you want to change.

Example: I want to change my negative thoughts about other people. I will run through a mental list of people in my circle of influence. I will think of all the positive attributes and characteristics of a person.

Set a timer for one minute. Make a mental note of both how many times you were successful with a positive focus on success and the times you were unfocused.

After one minute, log your focused attention and unfocused attention on a grid similar to the example on the following page.

Repeat this practice until you have completed ten timed minutes. Spend the last five minutes of the fifteen minutes you set aside to record your thoughts after the exercise.

A sample chart to record your focused thoughts might look similar to the following:

FOCUSED ATTENTION ON POSITIVE SUCCESS

Date: January 15th

Focus: Changing my negative thoughts about other people

MINUTE INTERVALS

Mark | for every time a thought (focused or unfocused) enters your mind.

Time: From ___ to ___	1	2	3	4	5	6	7	8	9	10
Focused Attention on Positive Success	‖‖‖ ‖‖‖ ‖	‖‖‖ ‖‖‖ ‖‖‖	‖‖‖ ‖‖‖ ‖‖‖ ‖	‖‖‖ ‖‖‖ ‖‖‖‖	‖‖‖ ‖‖‖ ‖‖‖ ‖‖‖	‖‖‖ ‖‖‖ ‖‖‖ ‖‖‖‖	‖‖‖ ‖‖‖ ‖‖‖ ‖‖‖ ‖	‖‖‖ ‖‖‖ ‖‖‖ ‖‖‖ ‖‖	‖‖‖ ‖‖‖ ‖‖‖ ‖‖‖ ‖‖‖	‖‖‖ ‖‖‖ ‖‖‖ ‖‖‖ ‖‖‖
Unfocused Attention	‖‖‖ ‖‖‖ ‖‖‖ ‖‖‖ ‖	‖‖‖ ‖‖‖ ‖‖‖ ‖‖	‖‖‖ ‖‖‖ ‖‖‖ ‖‖‖‖	‖‖‖ ‖‖‖‖	‖‖‖ ‖‖	‖‖‖ ‖	‖‖‖	‖‖	‖‖‖	

Practice this strategy daily for one week. Practicing every day is important. Compare your logs from each day.

As seen in the example above, you will see your own success with the practice as well as the areas that still require improvement. Then move on to the next strategy and extend the time of your practice from a week and beyond.

Using the example above, we can see that the individual was able to focus their attention on changing their negative thoughts about other people with a measure of success within the first fifteen minutes of making a mental list of people in their circle of influence. With each minute, they were increasingly more successful at thinking of positive attributes and characteristics of the people on their list one minute at a time.

For the next week, keep up with your daily plan, and add the practice of focusing on your next minute in real-life situations.

Focus on taking your newfound awareness of the issue you are working on, and put your focused attention on positive success into action.

Pick the best time of day to protect fifteen minutes for this mini-experiment.

Think about where you will be when you want to focus on what it is that you want to change. You might choose to a time when you and your significant other are taking care of a chore together or sharing a meal. You might pick a time when you are at work interacting with coworkers. It might be a time when you are driving home from work. Pick the time when you are most likely to experience the most challenge with the issue you are addressing.

Again, make sure your focus is on just one area that you desire to change at a time. Write your thoughts and experiences down at the end of each day for the week.

Example: I want to change my negative thoughts about other people while in the lunchroom at work. I will think of all the positive attributes and characteristics of each person who walks in the door to have lunch or whom I think of during lunchtime.

At the end of each week, note all the positive thoughts, words, and actions you have enacted in the functional setting and situations where you were able to focus your attention on positive success. Then focus on the barriers that presented themselves. Note those thoughts, words, and actions that stopped you from dealing with the targeted issue in a positive way.

Work on the same goal, or set new goals for yourself for the next week, continuing on for the next month, three months, six months, and year.

A sample chart to record your focused thoughts might look similar to the following grid:

FOCUSED ATTENTION ON POSITIVE SUCCESS
Date: January 22nd
Focus: Changing my negative thoughts about other people while at work
Place: Work lunchroom

MINUTE INTERVALS

Mark | for every time a thought (focused or unfocused) enters your mind.

Time: From____ to ____	1	2	3	4	5	6	7	8	9	10
Focused Attention on Positive Success	✝✝✝✝ ✝✝	✝✝✝✝ ✝✝✝✝ ✝✝✝	✝✝✝✝ ✝✝✝✝ ✝✝✝✝	✝✝✝✝ ✝✝✝✝ ✝✝✝✝ ✝	✝✝✝✝ ✝✝✝✝ ✝✝✝✝	✝✝✝✝ ✝✝✝✝ ✝✝✝✝ ✝✝✝	✝✝✝✝ ✝✝✝✝ ✝✝✝✝ ✝✝✝✝	✝✝✝✝ ✝✝✝✝ ✝✝✝✝ ✝✝✝✝	✝✝✝✝ ✝✝✝✝ ✝✝✝✝ ✝✝✝✝ ✝✝✝	✝✝✝✝ ✝✝✝✝ ✝✝✝✝ ✝✝✝✝ ✝✝✝
Unfocused Attention	✝✝✝✝ ✝✝✝✝ ✝✝✝✝ ✝✝✝✝	✝✝✝✝ ✝✝✝✝ ✝✝✝✝	✝✝✝✝ ✝✝✝✝ ✝✝✝	✝✝✝✝ ✝✝✝✝	✝✝✝✝ ✝✝✝✝	✝✝✝✝ ✝	✝✝✝✝		✝✝✝	✝✝✝✝ ✝✝✝✝ ✝✝✝✝

A Word of Caution: If success is not achieved, a regression is inevitable. *Regression means returning to the previous, less functioning state.* Resistance will resurface. The tendency is to want to close off from vulnerability and resume the old conviction that you are not accountable for your own personal expressions, growth, and success. Too, there is a tendency to take shortcuts, to gain a bit of knowledge and assume that you can be proficient with putting a new habit into practice right away. Well intended as you might be, rushing into the idea that change is complete without doing the work doesn't work. Rushing through the exercise too quickly is a recipe for disaster.

Time and practice are needed to achieve effective command over positively reinforcing change. Small steps toward change are required.

HOPELESS TO HAPPY

David wanted to know how many times in a day he showed up in his marriage like his father. He tried to figure out each behavior and then work on eliminating them one by one. He sat with Colleen and told her what he was going to work on and where he needed her help. It was the first time in three years they had talked calmly about the behaviors that weren't working for either of them in the marriage.

Together they came up with two behaviors for David to work on changing. David had a habit of dismissing Colleen when he was busy. She would ask if he could talk, and he would respond, "Not now," or "Can't you see I'm busy?" Colleen wouldn't say anything, but she would walk away feeling rejected and resentful. David also had the habit of coming home after work and complaining about his day. He unconsciously held the expectation that Colleen was to sit there and listen without making a comment. Colleen wanted to be supportive, but she struggled with his lack of reciprocity in a conversation. He did not appear to care about what she experienced in the day.

David woke early each day for a week. He took a quiet fifteen minutes before heading off to work. He thought about what he wanted to change. He came up with two behaviors he wanted to practice and positively reinforce.

When Colleen asked him if he could talk, he was going to stop what he was doing, put out his hand to hold hers and say, "Yes. What would you like to talk about?" The second behavior he was going to focus on was what he said when he first got home after work. He decided to proactively ask Colleen, "How was your day?" before he would say anything about his.

A month had passed. David and Colleen didn't talk directly about David's effort. But positive changes had occurred. David was making daily, concerted attempts to be available to Colleen when she wanted to talk and to ask her how her day was before talking about himself. Colleen started spending less time with her girlfriends and more time with him. No longer did David sense that Colleen was one foot out the door. He also felt successful at changing generational patterns passed down to him by his father.

David was the happiest he had been in his marriage ever. He was emotionally expressive. He spoke with animation and great smiles. For the first time in a long time, he felt hopeful. David was ready, after only one month, to tackle changing more undesirable behaviors to make his marriage even stronger.

PUTTING THE CHILDREN FIRST

Paulette and Howard were asked to define their priority over the next two weeks. Both stated that their children were their priority. The idea of creating a schedule of reinforcement was discussed to support the couple in keeping their priority. The couple was asked to create a reasonable plan to ensure their children remained a priority in their lives over the next two weeks and to help with the timing of when a reinforcer would be done.

Paulette pushed back. She said defensively, "I know what my kids need. I just gotta' make sure I take care of that."

"And what exactly do they need?" I asked.

Paulette went on to discuss all the things needed for the children from morning until night.

"So..." I continued, "if you know what they need, what is the barrier stopping them from having their needs met?"

"I get tired. I am so tired." Paulette started to cry. "I want some 'me' time. Howard is home all day, and he does nothing to help. I need help with cooking, cleaning, and caring for the kids. He does nothing!"

At that, Howard stiffened, "I don't know what to do. You always tell me to get away and let you do it! I see that you're tired, but you won't let me help, so I do my own thing." Tears welled up in his eyes.

As they sat there emotionally spent, I explained a simple *operant condition* strategy they could use to assist them throughout the day and in the coming weeks. The couple was ready to listen.

I shared that the two could benefit from setting up scheduled reinforcers. I explained that scheduling was an important component of the learning process as they began to change their behavior intentionally. I related that how often they reinforced a behavior could have a dramatic impact on the strength and rate of the desired positive response.

Then I asked Paulette and Howard to pull out their cell phones. I had them open up the alarm function on their clock apps. I counseled Howard to set his alarm for every hour at the top of the hour: seven o'clock, eight o'clock, nine o'clock, and so on. I asked Paulette to set her alarm for every half hour; six-thirty, seven-thirty, eight-thirty, and so on. Then I suggested that every hour on the hour Howard should shout out wherever he was in the house and proclaim, "The children are our priority!" Every half hour Paulette should shout out the same.

The couple was reluctant at first. They felt awkward blurting out the proclamations. But when the positive proclamations were held up against, and compared to, the shouts of profanity and cruelty previously being blurted out in the home, the couple let go of their resistance.

Then we added another step. Directly after Howard made his proclamations, he was to ask Paulette what he could do to help out around the house. And directly after Paulette made her proclamations, she was to let Howard know when she needed to take her next break.

Two weeks and a day had passed when I got a call from Paulette crying. This time, the tears were happy ones. She and Howard had gone to court that morning. They shared with the mediator, social worker, and judge the strategy they had put into place to ensure the children remained a priority in their lives. They shared their trials and ultimate successes. Howard took over laundry duties, cleaning the bathrooms, and making sure the floors were clean and the carpet was vacuumed. Paulette found that two fifteen-minute breaks in the day, one in the morning and one in the afternoon, were enough of a break from her children. The couple hadn't had a single fight while they focused on working together to make their children their priority.

The judge had allowed the children to remain in the home. Social Services would still be randomly checking up on them, yet, for now, they stayed together as a family.

MAKE IT A HABIT
FOCUS ON SMALL SUCCESSES
STEPS FOR SUCCESS

EXERCISE 1:
A DAILY PLAN

Pick the best time of day to have a quiet fifteen minutes to complete this task. Think about what you want to focus on to positively reinforce.

During this time think about that one thing you would like to change. Make sure your focus is on just one area. Write your thoughts down. Each day for one week, take ten minutes to focus your attention on what you want to change.

Set a timer for one minute. Take a mental note of both how many times you were successful with positive focus and the times you were unfocused. After one minute, log your focused attention and unfocused attention on the blank graph on the next page.

Repeat this practice until you have completed ten timed minutes.

Practice this strategy every day for one week. It is important to practice every day. Compare your daily logs. You will begin to see your own success with the practice, as well as, the areas that still require improvement. Then move on to the next exercise.

Remember not to allow resistance to deter you. Do not close yourself off from vulnerability. You are accountable for your own personal expressions, growth, and success. Also, do not take shortcuts, and assume that you can be proficient with putting a new habit into practice right away.

Real change takes patience and consistency over a prolonged period of time..

FOCUSED ATTENTION ON POSITIVE SUCCESS
Date:_____

Focus:_____

MINUTE INTERVALS
Mark **l** for every time a thought (focused or unfocused) enters your mind.

Time: From_____ to _____	1	2	3	4	5	6	7	8	9	10
Focused Attention on Positive Success										
Unfocused Attention										

EXERCISE 2: WEEKLY PLAN

For the next week, keep up with your daily plan. Add the practice of focusing on your next minute in real-life situations. Focus on taking your newfound awareness of the issue you are working on and put your focused attention on positive success into action.

Pick the best time of day to protect fifteen minutes for this mini-experiment. Think about where you will be when you want to focus on what it is that you want to change. You might choose a time when you and your significant other are taking care of a chore together or sharing a meal. You might pick a time when you are at work interacting with coworkers. It might be a time when you are riding home from work. Pick the time when you are most likely to experience the most challenge with the issue you are addressing.

FOCUSED ATTENTION ON POSITIVE SUCCESS Date:_____										
Focus:_____										
Place:_____										
MINUTE INTERVALS *Mark	for every time a thought (focused or unfocused) enters your mind.*										
Time: From_____ to _____	1	2	3	4	5	6	7	8	9	10
Focused Attention on Positive Success										
Unfocused Attention										

Again, make sure your focus is on just one area that you desire to change at a time. Write your thoughts and experiences down at the end of each day for the week.

At the end of the week, note all the positive thoughts, words, and actions you have enacted in the functional setting and situations where you were able to focus your attention on positive success. Then focus on the barriers that presented themselves. Note those thoughts, words, and actions that stopped you from dealing with the targeted issue in a positive way.

Work on the same goal, or set new goals for yourself for the next week.

EXERCISE 3: MONTHLY PLAN

Each month continue on with the above exercise. Take extra time to look back at the volume of entries. What patterns do you observe? Has it been easy to write for an entire month? Did you miss days of writing? What are some of the consistent personal strengths you are aware of that were not so obvious before? Is there a pattern of successes? A pattern of barriers?

By giving focused attention on a targeted issue, change regarding that issue naturally occurs. What changes have you observed about yourself? What changes have you observed specifically about the issue of focus?

Practice this exercise for three months, six months, and a year. See what becomes of thoughts, words, and actions regarding the targeted issue after that amount of time.

CONCLUSION

I have compiled these ten communication strategies for the intended purpose of helping you connect more fully with loved ones and to restore any communication that may be damaged. The strategies are simple and straightforward. They are designed to help you put them into daily practice, using minimal effort. The idea is that you can access a measure of success the first time you try a strategy. Experiencing success will most likely compel you to use the strategies again and again.

Communication is learned and requires practice. Skillful communication is vital in relationships. Most individuals and couples can develop this skill and learn how to communicate more effectively. The process involves the ongoing practice of you and your partner or spouse sending and receiving thoughts, ideas, and information in a mutual interchange with the common goal of understanding and valuing each other's messages.

Start small and increase your communication skills. Keep your perspective as you actively listen. Verbalize thoughts and ideas with new-found openness and safety. Let go of having to control the exchange. Become curious about the most loving way to embrace a new idea or problem solve together. You and your partner or spouse are more important than any problem you will face. Be clear with your boundaries. Remain motivated to continually develop your communication skills. Make healthy choices leading to positive habit formation. Lastly, focus on your small successes toward skillful communication.

To your success!

—Denise Healy—

REFERENCES

CHAPTER 1

1. On Becoming a Person: A Therapist's View of Psychotherapy. Carl R. Rogers, Houghton Mifflin Company, 1961, 1989, 1995.

2. A Way of Being. Carl R. Rogers, Introduction by Irvin D. Yalom, Houghton Mifflin Company, 1995 reprint of 1980 Edition.

3. Client-Centered Therapy: Its Current Practice, Implications, and Theory. Carl R. Rogers, Houghton Mifflin, 1951, digitized 2008.

4. Active Listening. Carl R. Rogers and Richard Evans, Martino Publishing, 2015 reprint of 1943 Edition.

5. A Theory of Human Motivation. Abraham H. Maslow, Rough Draft Printing, 2013 reprint of 1943 Edition.

6. Motivation and Personality. Abraham H. Maslow, Harper & Brothers, 1954.

7. Using Standardized Clients in the Classroom: An Evaluation of a Training Module to Teach Active Listening Skills to Social Work Students. Anissa Rogers, Ph.D. and Benjamin Welch, Journal of Teaching in Social Work, Taylor & Francis, Published online: 03 Apr 2009.

CHAPTER 2

1. The Language and Thought of the Child. Jean Piaget, Routledge: London, 2001.

2. Mind in Society: The Development of Higher Psychological Processes. L. S. Vygotsky, Harvard University Press, 1978.

3. The Centrality of Language in Human Cognition, Language Learning. Gary Lupyan, Wiley Online Library, https://onlinelibrary.wiley.com, 2015.

CHAPTER 3

1. A Novel Neural Prediction Error Found in Anterior Cingulate Cortex Ensembles. James Michael Hyman, Clay Brian Holroyd, Jeremy Keith Seamans. Neuron, http://dx.doi.org/10.1016/j.neuron.2017.06.021, 2017.

2. Contemplative Practices and Mental Training: Prospects for American Education Mind and Life Education Research Network (MLERN). Richard J. Davidson et al; University of Wisconsin, Emory University, University of Michigan, Mind and Life Institute, Pennsylvania State University, University of Miami, Institute of Tibetan Classics, Inner Resilience Program, Portland State University, and Harvard Medical School; Child Development Perspectives, Volume 6, Number 2, 2012.

3. Amygdala and Ventromedial Prefrontal Cortex Are Inversely Coupled During Regulation of Negative Affect and Predict the Diurnal Pattern of Cortisol Secretion among Older Adults. Urry et al., Journal of Neuroscience, 19 Apr 2006.

4. Dynamic Development of Psychological Structures in Action and Thought. K. W. Fischer, T. R. Bidell, In: D. W. and R. M. Lerner (Editors), Handbook of child psychology, 5th Edition, Volume 1: Theoretical models of human development; Wiley, 1998.

CHAPTER 4

1. Edward Thorndike. S. A. McLeod, http://www.simplypsychology.org/edward-thorndike.html, 2016.

2. Conditioned Reflexes: An Investigation of the Physiological Activity of the Cerebral Cortex. Ivan P. Pavlov, Oxford University Press, 1927.

3. Burrhus Frederick Skinner: The Contingencies of a Life. D. W. Bjork, In: G. A. Kimble and M. Wertheimer (Editors), Portraits of Pioneers in Psychology, 1991.

4. Episodic Future Thinking and Episodic Counterfactual Thinking: Intersections Between Memory and Decisions. D. L. Schacter, R. G. Benoit, F. DeBrigard, K. K. Szpunar, Neurobiology of Learning and Memory, 2015.

5. Episodic Future Thinking. C. M. Atance, D. K. O'Neill, Trends in Cognitive Sciences, Cell Press, 01 Dec 2001.

6. Episodic Future Thought: An Emerging Concept. K. K. Szpunar, Perspectives on Psychological Science, Sage Publications, Mar 2010.

7. Influence of Outcome Valence in the Subjective Experience of Episodic Past, Future, and Counterfactual Thinking. F. DeBrigard, K. S. Giovanello, Consciousness and Cognition, Sage Publications, Sep 2012.

CHAPTER 5

1. Maternal Care and Mental Health. J. Bowlby, World Health Organization Monograph (Serial No. 2), 1951.

Attachment and Loss, Volume 1, Attachment. J. Bowlby, Basic Books, 1969.

Attachment and Loss, Volume 2, Separation: Anxiety and Anger. J. Bowlby, Basic Books, 1973.

Attachment and Loss, Volume 3, Loss: Sadness and Depression. J. Bowlby, Basic Books, 1980.

A Secure Base. J. Bowlby. Basic Books, 1988.

2. Some Considerations Regarding Theory and Assessment Relevant to Attachments Beyond Infancy. M. D. S. Ainsworth, In: M. T. Greenberg, D. Cicchetti, and E. M. Cummings (Editors), Attachment in the Preschool Years: Theory, Research, and Intervention, University of Chicago Press, 1990.

Patterns of Attachment: A Psychological Study of the Strange Situation. M. D. S. Ainsworth, M. Blehar, E. Waters, and S. Wall, Lawrence Erlbaum, 1978.

3. Adult Romantic Attachment: Theory and Evidence. P. R. Shaver, and C. Hazan, Advances in Personal Relationships, Jessica Kingsley Publishers Ltd., 1993.

4. Adult Attachment, Working Models, and Relationship Quality in Dating Couples. Nancy L. Collins, Stephen J. Read, Journal of Personality and Social Psychology, Volume 58, Number 4, American Psychological Association, 1990.

5. The Fantasy Bond: Structure of Psychological Defenses. Robert W. Firestone, Ph.D., Human Sciences Press/Insight Books 1985; The Glendon Association, 1999.

6. Adult Attachment Insecurity and Hippocampal Cell Density. M. Quirin, O. Gillath, J. C. Pruessner, L. D. Eggert, Social Cognition and Affective Neuroscience, Oxford University Press, Mar 2010.

7. What's Inside the Minds of Securely and Insecurely Attached People? The Secure-Base Script and its Associations with Attachment-Style Dimensions. M. Mikulincer, P. R. Shaver, Y. Sapir-Lavid, and N. Avihou-Kanza, Journal of Personality and Social Psychology, American Psychological Association, 2009.

CHAPTER 6

1. Boundaries Updated and Expanded Edition: When to Say Yes, How to Say No to Take Control of Your Life. Dr. Henry Cloud and Dr. John Townsend, Zondervan, 2017.

2. What Do You Mean 'Boundaries'?. Dr. Henry Cloud and Dr. John Townsend, Zondervan, 2016.

3. Boundaries are the limits and rules we set for ourselves within relationships. Marvin G. Knittel, Ed.D, https://www.psychologytoday.com/us/blog/how-help-friend/201711/why-is-it-important-have-personal-boundaries, Published online: 17 Nov 2017.

4. Setting Boundaries with Difficult People: Six Steps to Sanity for Challenging Relationships. Allison Bottke, Harvest House Publishers, 2011.

5. Setting Boundaries with Negative Thoughts and Painful Memories: How to Stop Hoarding Your Hurts. Allison Bottke, Harvest House Publishers, 2017.

CHAPTER 7

1. Self-Efficacy: Toward a Unifying Theory of Behavioral Change. A. Bandura, Educational Psychology Review, Springer Science+Business Media, 1977.

2. Achievement Motivation and Memory: Achievement Goals Differentially Influence Immediate and Delayed Remember-Know Recognition Memory. K. Murayama, A. J. Elliot, Personality and Social Psychology Bulletin, Sage Publishing, 2011.

3. Motivational Process Affects Learning. C. S. Dweck, http://dx.doi.org/10.1037/0003-066X.41.10, American Psychologist, 1986.

CHAPTER 8

1. Taxonomy of Educational Objectives, Handbook 1: Cognitive Domain. Benjamin S. Bloom, David McKay Company, 1966.

2. Action in Perception. Alva Noe, MIT Press, 2004.

CHAPTER 9

1. The Pull of the Past: When Do Habits Persist Despite Conflict with Motives?. D. T. Neal, W. Wood, W., M. Wu, and D. Kurlander, Personality and Social Psychology Bulletin, Volume 37, Sage Publishing, 2011.

2. Automaticity: A Theoretical and Conceptual Analysis. A. Moors, and J. De Houwer, Psychological Bulletin, Volume 132, American Psychological Association, 2006.

3. Experiences of Habit Formation: A Qualitative Study. P. Lally, J. Wardle, B. Gardner; Psychology, Health & Medicine, Published online: 16 Aug 2011.

4. Making Health Habitual: The Psychology of 'Habit Formation' and General Practice. P. Lally, J. Wardle, B. Gardner, British Journal of General Practice (BJGP), Dec 2012.

CHAPTER 10

1. Conditioned Reflexes (Classics of Psychology), Ivan P. Pavlov, Amazon Kindle eBook, Revised 24 May 2013.

2. About Behaviorism. Burrhus Frederic Skinner, Vintage Books, 1974.

ABOUT THE AUTHOR

Denise Healy is an author, relationship expert, and co-founder and co-CEO of Streets2Schools, Inc. As a victim's advocate who works with violent offenders, Denise has developed successful strategies for mending broken connections in all types of relationships. Denise has taught, mentored, coached, and counseled thousands of people over the course of her career, and holds master's degrees in educational leadership, psychology, and school psychology.

Denise adds value to people by assisting them in applying positive social skills strategies to real life circumstances which lead to positive outcomes and success. She is also the author of a children's book on managing emotions, **Christopher's Anger,** and a contributing author to the book, **Success Formula,** with Jack Canfield.

For more information about Denise, her books and training programs, visit *DeniseHealy.com* and *streets2schools.com*.

DEAR READER

Thank you for reading *Mending Broken Connections*, I hope you enjoyed it as much as I enjoyed writing it. Won't you please consider leaving a review on the page or site where you bought the book? Even just a few words would help others decide if the book is right for them.

Best regards and thank you in advance,

Denise Healy

NOTES

Made in the USA
Monee, IL
06 October 2020